Praise

'Finally, the playbook we've all been craving! Trends, insights, culture shifts – the root of all great ideas. Because let's be real: brilliant ideas don't grow on trees; they are shaped by what's happening *right now*. This book connects the dots between creativity and culture in way that just makes sense. It goes beyond defining trends, it gets under the skin of them. How to use them, and how to land them with confidence to deliver what people actually want. Because that's the goal, right? To lead, not follow. Feeley's nailed it. Sharp, insightful, energising and motivating. I'm grabbing copies for my team – it's a must-read for every creative and marketeer who is serious about staying relevant, resonant and ahead of the curve.'
  — **Emma Baines**, Global Head of Creative, Tony's Chocolonely

'If you run a business, you need this book. It makes one thing crystal clear, your future depends on your ability to understand your future customer. If you don't yet have a trend leader in your company, this book will show you why that role is not a luxury but a necessity. If you do, give them this book – your future customer will thank you.'
  — **Karen Haller**, Behavioural Colour and Design Psychology, and author of *The Little Book of Colour*

'Joanna's insights on trend leadership have been a turning point in my personal and professional journey. Trends are a vast, ever-changing world and, at times, can be intimidating. The tips in this book provided me with the tools to lead and inspire my colleagues to connect with consumers in a more meaningful way, while also giving me a better understanding of the world we live in and helping me find my purpose. On my journey as a trend leader, I've learned valuable lessons that have boosted my confidence in decision making, strengthened my assertiveness and shaped my professional career as a leader.'
— **Diego Sancho**, Character Design Manager, The LEGO Group

'An inspiring and practical guide for anyone looking to lead future-focused conversations with confidence. Drawing on her incredible experience spanning over twenty-five years, Jo Feeley demystifies trend forecasting through six clear principles, real-world case studies and actionable tools. Her expertise shines through in every chapter, empowering professionals – regardless of background – to become confident trend leaders who drive meaningful change. Whether you're new to trends or ready to elevate your influence, this is a must-read for anyone looking to futureproof their decisions, spark innovation and build a stronger, more responsive organisation.'
— **Sarah-Jane Porter**, Design and Licensing Director, Moonpig

'This new book offers organisations the opportunity to gain exceptional insights from a well-respected expert in the field of evaluating and setting trends, Joanna Feeley. I'd recommend it to anyone seeking ways to innovate and anticipate trends to stay ahead of the field and gain competitive advantage, whether in the commercial or not-for-profit sector. For me, the main highlights include the sections on reflecting and taking action in relation to trends, as well as real-life cases from experienced trend specialists. These perspectives advance the discussion on trends for the benefit of readers from both industry and academia.'
— **Helen Goworek**, Professor in Marketing, Durham University Business School

'I've known Jo and TrendBible since their early days and watched the business develop and grow. Once we started working together commercially, I found no other person or service offered their unique approach while delivering tangible success and outcomes. Quite simply, Jo has nailed trend forecasting and cultivated her insights and experience into a universal, compelling and effective method for any business or category. This book gives you your own magic crystal ball, making trend forecasting clear and relevant for everyone to use. Whether you are a creative, marketeer, researcher, strategist or business manager, I wholly recommend this book.'
— **Geoff Sanderson**, Founder of Jungle Studio and former Creative Director at Moonpig and Hallmark

Trend Leader

How to spot and
back winning ideas
to accelerate your
career and create
a better future

Joanna Feeley

R^ethink

First published in Great Britain in 2025
by Rethink Press (www.rethinkpress.com)

© Copyright Joanna Feeley

Exclamation Mark icon by Elisabeta from Noun Project (CC BY 3.0)

This book is dedicated to Aidan and Cameron,
with love, whatever your future holds.

To Emma,
keep spotting the
signals others miss!

Joanne.
b

Contents

Introduction

Throughout my career as a trend forecaster, I've advised many global organisations and helped them understand what consumers will think, feel and do in the future.

Often, this means working with managers and leaders who are completely new to the world of trend forecasting. They find themselves accountable for making important decisions that impact the business in two to five years' time, but with no clear idea of what their audience's lives will look like by then. By teaching them how to use trends, I have helped them future-proof their decisions and position themselves as trend leaders who are responsible for holding conversations about the future.

So first, what is a trend leader? As far as I'm aware, there is no specific job title 'trend leader'. It's a term I use to describe people who ascend into a role in which they are responsible for trends, usually while working in a management position in design, product development, brand management, marketing or consumer research.

The good news is that you don't need to be a trend expert to drive important change in your company. If you are a business leader or manager and don't know where or how to begin introducing trends to your organisation, this book is for you. It's a guide to help you discuss trends with confidence. Learning how to use trends can make a real difference to your business and your customers, and it can help you level up in your career, too.

Perhaps you are working inside one of the many companies that doesn't have a person nominated to keep an eye on the future, or you're working for one of the 66% of companies that doesn't have a dedicated internal foresight department.[1] Or perhaps you can simply sense the pace at which the world is changing, and you're worried that your business isn't keeping up.

In the coming years, there will be a growing interest in future-focused disciplines like trend forecasting and

---

1   F Buder, *The Value of Foresight in a VUCA World* (Nuremberg Institute for Market Decisions, 2021), www.nim.org/fileadmin/PUBLIC/3_NIM_Publikationen/NIM_Research_Reports/the_value_of_foresight_in_a_vuca_world_v3.pdf, accessed 12 May 2025

strategic foresight[2] as more companies crave the security they offer, enabling them to make robust decisions that withstand complex change. An increasingly broad range of companies feel they simply cannot risk missing what's changing for their customer – whether they make cat food or washing machines.

The world's most successful brands and retailers rely heavily on systems for understanding trends. After all, you can't develop a company strategy, plan future product ranges or sign off new marketing campaigns if you don't know what social mood awaits you.

A trend leader needs to have a clear understanding of what's changing over the coming years, including how social and cultural trends and shifting market dynamics will impact the future consumers' beliefs, values, choices and tastes. Consumers don't make their decisions in a vacuum; they are shaped by what's happening in the world around them. Trend leaders help businesses anticipate and prepare for changes that are coming by creating a trend forecast that's tailored to their company and market. They activate trends and bring them to life through positioning the brand, products and marketing campaigns in a way that appeals to the future attitudes and behaviours of the consumer.

Being able to prompt quality conversations about the future and help organisations adapt to change are going to be among the most desirable leadership qualities

---

2   For a full glossary of terms, head to www.trendbible.com/trend-resources

over the next decade. Trend forecasting is an essential skill that is in high demand, and is being woven into corporate decision making. This isn't just about predicting market directions – it's about creating a *preferred* future that aligns with your audience's deepest values and aspirations. Businesses will thrive by being more responsive to the changing needs of their environment, stakeholders and the wider community.

As part of my research, I've interviewed many trend leaders who have shared their wisdom, learnings and skills across a broad range of industries. In this book, you'll hear about the impact they have had on the lives of others. You'll meet the people behind ideas such as 'Thinking of You Week', a widely celebrated occasion for telling your loved ones they matter, through to someone whose on-the-go laundry invention went on an expedition to the International Space Station to help astronauts do their laundry.

Part One of this book, clarifies what trends are and what role they play in a progressive company. It also digs into the results of a behavioural study examining the skills and behaviours of trend leaders.

While there's absolutely something to be learned from the people running large foresight divisions in some of the world's biggest brands, some of the sharpest lessons come from trend leaders who have had few resources available to them and haven't always had the backing of a senior leadership team. Yet they have still managed to create a picture of the future for their businesses and drive important commercial and social change.

As well as the behavioural study and expert interviews conducted for this book, I've condensed over twenty-five years' of knowledge and observations from advising those new to trends into six guiding principles of trend leadership, intended to demystify the trend forecasting process and give you access to practical tools and strategies that you can apply in your business today.

These are covered in Part Two, where we'll explore each guiding principle in detail:

- **Principle 1:** Create a trend framework. Understand how to develop a roadmap to transform ideas and concepts into tangible outputs that reach your audience in time.

- **Principle 2:** Hold space for curiosity and challenge. Learn how to have the right conversations with the right people inside your organisation.

- **Principle 3:** Gather trend intelligence. Access the right resources to help you feel informed. Discover how to use trends to support your decisions and be sure you're backing a winning idea.

- **Principle 4:** Contextualise your trends – how to build robustness into your decision making to ensure your trends land well with your audience.

- **Principle 5:** Validate your trends. Create a clear rationale for the decisions you make and compile an evidence file to track and monitor a trend's emergence.

- **Principle 6:** Build belief. Develop the confidence to take ownership of the conversation around trends and become an in-demand trend leader. Articulate your future vision to your colleagues and stakeholders and drive change.

Each chapter concludes with reflection and action points to help you embed and execute each of these principles.

Alongside the six guiding principles in this book, you'll also be able to evaluate your current trend leadership status, mark your progress towards each of the six principles using our Trend Leader Assessment Tool, and pinpoint areas for development to drive your own trend leadership over on my website – www.joannafeeley.com – or simply scan the QR code at the end of this book to unlock access.

Throughout my career, I have helped people without any trend-forecasting skills thrive using these methods. My hope is that, after reading this book, you won't feel quite so intimidated about using trends and that you'll be equipped to start a future-focused conversation that drives important change in your business.

PART ONE
UNDERSTANDING WHAT TRENDS ARE, WHY THEY MATTER AND WHAT A TREND LEADER IS

ONE

The Importance Of Trends In A Progressive Company

Progressive companies don't wait for their customers' lives to change before they react; they anticipate change years in advance by dedicating time and resources to thinking about future trends. In this chapter, we will clarify the definition of a trend, and how companies use trends to stay relevant for their audience. We'll uncover why it's important to think about the needs of your future customer, not just your current one, and how to align future trends with the goals and ambitions of your business to create meaningful change.

What are trends and why do they matter?

There are multiple definitions of a trend, but in its simplest form, a trend is an expression of change. The way we live our lives, the choices we make, the things we are drawn to – whether that's a certain make of car or a blanket in a new colour – are all anticipated and prepared for years in advance by the brands and retailers we buy from. In fact, it goes much deeper than that: the future is actively and formally planned for by the policy makers who shape our society, and the culture makers who curate the exhibitions and films we'll see in two – or five or ten – years' time. Why are they so keen to look that far ahead, and how do they know what we'll want two or more years from now?

Trend forecasting helps businesses:

- Anticipate consumers' wants and needs

- Inform and validate strategic decisions

- Drive innovation

- Guide brand and marketing

- Mitigate risks

- Adapt to market changes and react to emerging opportunities

In commercial terms, looking ahead is a way of pre-empting demand. Being prepared for shifts in taste and being in a position to take advantage of them is appealing to companies who have product design and manufacturing cycles that can span several years. They simply can't 'magic up' a product in a few weeks – it takes time and energy to produce and engineer it, and so having confidence that their product will be popular in a future context is reassuring.

A strong grasp of future trends enables brands and organisations to better understand what their consumer will do next so they can make more informed decisions in the here and now, a practice adopted by some of the world's biggest brands, such as Target:

> 'As a retailer that serves millions of consumers every day, we understand the importance of staying in step with the evolving external landscape, now and in the future.'[3]

It's as much about *not getting it wrong* as it is about getting it right – no company wants to be lumbered with stock that didn't sell or face questions about the cost of a marketing campaign that didn't land well with their target audience.

To give you an example, fast-food giant McDonald's transitioned to using paper drinking straws (from the 1.8 million plastic ones they use daily in the UK) back in 2018. They made the shift ahead of a forthcoming legislative change driven by environmental concerns, which resulted in a UK government ban on single-use plastics in 2020. McDonald's early actions did not result in an immediate success – paper straws were more expensive to produce than plastic ones, and they experienced customer criticism for the quality and taste, which led to an extended innovation

---

3 N Meyersohn, 'Target is the latest company to roll back some DEI programs', *CNN Business* (24 January 2025), https://edition.cnn.com/2025/01/24/business/target-dei-companies/index.html, accessed 9 April 2025

process to create a better alternative – but had they not acted early and pre-empted change, getting over these unforeseen stumbling blocks could have taken them beyond the government deadline where they would have faced fines, reputational damage and legal repercussions.

Being able to see the changes coming beyond the horizon goes much further than simply reading up on forthcoming legislation. Trends are informed by all sorts of changes in the world around us.

Change is a constant, and it's usually a deep understanding of this fact that motivates a progressive business to commission a trend partner to help keep them abreast of the huge amount of change that's happening at any given time. Even companies that invest in having their own internal foresight teams still commission trend intelligence from independent trend agencies to gain an external perspective. Outsourcing your trend forecasting enables you to stay sufficiently 'zoomed out' to see the bigger picture, as you'll likely be juggling trends alongside product development, managing your direct reports and working towards a divisional strategy among other things.

Though I'd always recommend that you are personally plugged in to what's changing (subscribing to a diverse range of newsletters, reading books, listening to podcasts, reading white papers, attending global trade shows and synthesising your research and thinking from all of these sources), as a mid- to senior-level manager inside a large organisation, you will only be able to devote so many hours a week to these activities. Accurate trend forecasting requires constant monitoring and updating.

Regardless of the source of trend information, progressive companies work to a future trend forecast that tells them where change is coming from and why, what the impact of this will be on customer mindset and behaviour, and when it will hit peak relevance.

This book is not intended to teach you how to go about the detailed and time-consuming process of learning how to forecast trends from scratch yourself. I know from experience that it takes at least two years to train a university graduate in even the basics of trend research, let alone connecting the dots from research to future forecasting. The intention of this is book is to teach you how to access published trend intelligence and understand enough about trends to use it inside your business to drive change.

To keep it simple, I recommend focusing on what is changing across three main knowledge areas. A good trend forecast should provide you with a clear picture of the future and a specific timeframe on:

1. Future consumer lifestyle: pre-empting changes in how people will be living

2. Future consumer mindset: pre-empting shifts in the beliefs, experiences and emotions that will inform consumer mindset

3. Product innovation: design, material, ingredient and manufacturing innovation that informs what it is possible to create

Putting the future customer first

I've met some brilliant businesses doing so many things right, but they get tripped up by one thing – not knowing enough about their future customer. Once they realise that they don't have a handle on how their customer is changing, they start to look for solutions. Sometimes, they commission market research or conduct customer insight focus groups, only to find that this just gives them a static picture of their customer *today*. While this is useful, it doesn't do the job of investigating what will be different for your customers in the coming months or years. Clarity and understanding of the future customer are the main outputs of the discipline of trend forecasting.

The customer is always at the centre of a company's decision making, but many only study how their customer lives in the present. Thinking about the future customer enables you to identify both how your existing customers are changing, and who your prospective customers might be down the road. It's worth taking a moment to reflect on what work your company has done recently to better understand your future customer.

It's critical for trend leaders to view the world through the eyes of their future customer, because the change that's coming is significant and complex and requires companies to be well informed.

Progressive companies are realising that reputational improvements must be made if they are to capture the attention of progressive consumers, who increasingly bring their ethics and values to every purchasing decision they make. It's no longer enough to serve up convenience or low cost to a customer that's concerned with issues like fair pay for workers, inequality and environmental harm.

As a trend leader, you are part of a group of decision makers responsible for creating a balanced dynamic between commercial success, connecting with your customer and, I would argue, shouldering the responsibility that all companies should feel to make a positive societal impact.

Businesses play a huge part in how we drive positive change. They are considered *the* most trusted institutions – more so than governments or the media – both in general terms and when it comes to introducing new innovations into society.[4] Such trust creates real power for companies, but it will only be sustained if it is met with a desire to shoulder the responsibility.

---

4   Edelman, *2024 Edelman Trust Barometer Reveals Innovation Has Become a New Risk Factor for Trust* (2024), www.edelman.com/news-awards/2024-edelman-trust-barometer, accessed 9 April 2025

It's tempting to believe that the issues we face as a species, like global warming or the depletion of natural resources, are so vast that no single person can do much about reversing them. You are quite probably working for a company that contributes towards making this worse. Thankfully, you, and thousands of people like you, in a position of authority inside a global brand, want to make things better. It's probably one of the reasons why you picked up this book in the first place.

There are some pretty ugly stories about how products are designed, manufactured, marketed, used and discarded, and the role of corporations in this cycle is up for review.

To give a few examples, 300 million litres of paint go to landfill in Europe each year and 1.9 million tonnes of paint end up in our oceans every year. In the US, 18 million mattresses go to landfill each year. Singapore's landfill space may run out altogether by 2035. Air pollution kills 6.7 million people each year and is projected to become the top cause of environmentally related deaths worldwide by 2050. The numbers are staggering.

In the face of such a devastating impact, the world needs more original ideas, and futures tools – like trend forecasting and foresight – are essential for unlocking them. The discipline of trend forecasting helps us map and illustrate the world that future audiences will live in. It helps us identify how people will think and feel and what they'll be drawn towards. It helps us not only make sense of the bigger events that impact our lives, like elections and technological innovation, but also the small, subtle motivating factors that nudge our tastes and behaviours. The discipline of strategic foresight takes us beyond what we know of 'now' and helps us imaginatively explore what could happen next, helping us choose a better way and articulate a *preferred* future.

When businesses use these tools to create a 'forward view' that works for them, works for their future customer, and works for the planet, they fit a new definition of what it means to be successful; they are celebrated and loved for being relevant and meaningful. Increasingly, consumers and stakeholders are looking to measure a company's commitment to purpose beyond profit, with annual studies like the Purpose Power Index spotlighting the practices of over 200 brands.

The fact is that companies must do better. Society is asking them to do better. To be cleaner, greener, more transparent, fairer. Companies are being asked to do good in exchange for taking up so much space and having done so much harm.

Our actions today will shape the narratives of tomorrow, but is your company focused on the right things?

What does a better future look like for your company?

It's critical to understand what kind of future your company is striving for. Is the plan simply to satisfy shareholders? Move into new markets? Diversify your offering? Reach carbon zero? Attract a new audience?

Whatever its goal, if it doesn't also reflect what's happening in the world, it will lack relevance, as Richard Dickson, former custodian of the ever-enduring doll brand Barbie noted:

> 'In our sixty-year history, if you ever see dips in the brand's performance there was a clear disconnect between our messaging and what was happening at the time. When we create product, promotions and messaging that are a reflection of what is happening in the world, the brand maintains its presence, and we enjoy growth.'[5]

In a progressive business (and by progressive, I mean that it doesn't plan on standing still and that there is an appetite to thrive, not merely survive), everyone cares about what the customer will do next, and each person has a role to play in serving them. The most

---

5   R Dickson quoted in M Fleming, 'Mattel's marketing boss on giving Barbie a timely makeover', *Marketing Week* (11 December 2018), www.marketingweek.com/barbie-makeover-60th-birthdayerg, accessed 9 April 2025

successful companies I've worked with treat future preparedness as a strategic objective. For them, mapping the future is an industry-leading activity, essential for creating plans that drive competitive advantage. In these businesses, you can see the discipline of trend forecasting run through the whole organisation, from the strategic decision makers on the executive team (whose job it is to futureproof the business and understand the context in which it will be operating), right through to product teams, designers and marketing.

These companies understand that devoting time, resources and budget to thinking about the future is vital.

It is great to see foresight being taken so seriously among the world's most successful businesses, but according to the World Economic Forum, 75% of organisations are not prepared for the pace of change in their industry.[6]

Too often, a business's strategic vision is overly focused on financial metrics, or predicted changes within the immediate market and competitor landscape, without integrating a more holistic view of the opportunities the future holds. It's rarely connected to what the future consumer will be thinking, feeling and doing.

---

6 P Carvalho and O Woeffray, *The Future Isn't What It Used to Be: Here's How Strategic Foresight Can Help* (WEF, 2023), www.weforum.org/agenda/2023/02/strategic-intelligence-why-foresight-key-future-readiness, accessed 9 April 2025

For a business to enjoy a better future, senior leaders must ensure that it not only meets the immediate expectations of shareholders, but that it also considers the evolving demands and values of future consumers over the next two to five years. Ideally, they will plan towards a broader timeframe that takes into consideration the long-term legacy the company is driving.

There is a dangerous line of thought that a company devoting time and resources to thinking about the future is actively taking away from the more pressing problems it faces in the here and now. This is an unhelpful mindset that gets in the way of driving real change and one that can perpetually keep you locked in firefighting mode, which, while this may be within the realm of some people's roles, is not the purpose of a future thinker inside an organisation.

So, has there been a clear articulation of what a better future looks like for your business? Are you clear on where the company thinks it's headed, and have the vision, mission and values been communicated across the business?

The rise of forecasting across new sectors

Forecasting trends is a well-established practice in the military, oil and gas, automotive and fashion industries, but it's brand new in others. Over my career, I have seen an increasing number of industries wake up to the benefits of understanding the future.

In fact, I founded my own trend-forecasting business, TrendBible, in anticipation of this rise. In 2006, I spotted an opportunity to provide trends for new sectors after predicting a big lifestyle shift: that consumers would spend more time at home.

My hypothesis was validated as emerging signals of change began to unfold in the UK – nightclubs began closing their doors as younger audiences chose instead to stay at home, enticed by the hugely improved quality and availability of cinematic home entertainment that saw newly established Netflix hit its first £1 billion in revenue in 2007. At the same time, supermarkets began producing alcohol that was much cheaper to consume at home than in bars. Even our appetite for interiors changed – an open-plan, kitchen-living design became the most sought-after home renovation project that meant cooking, socialising and relaxing blended in a 'one space' environment that prompted a new way of being together. Previously, if you'd wanted to watch something other than what was on the family TV, you'd have to leave the room and go elsewhere, but now families could co-exist in these single spaces, firing up multiple screens from iPads to smartphones in addition to the traditional TV.

Even the food we ate and how we ate it changed. In place of home cooking came the popularisation of home delivery services, with Just Eat establishing its headquarters in London in 2006, and, later, the launch of their rival Deliveroo in 2013, which subsequently drove them to unicorn status, floating on the London

Stock Exchange by the time this trend peaked. In 2009, the Hummingbird Bakery Cookbook was published to huge acclaim making baking so cool that, by 2010, the BBC commissioned its most popular cookery show ever, *The Great British Bake Off.*

Social media also amplified this trend in which home was considered the new epicentre of our lives, and when Instagram launched as the first platform with a focus on imagery in 2010, users could visually express their tastes and personalities in a whole new way. Sharing photos of their home style (which previously had only been seen by close family and friends) could now be shared widely as the ultimate status symbol, where once fashion had dominated as the main medium of self-expression.

I watched my prediction come true, one signal at a time, as 'home' became a hugely important place in consumers' lives. As the trend grew, more companies found themselves impacted – in good and bad ways – by this significant lifestyle transformation. How and what people cooked, how they cohabited, socialised and interacted, and what items defined their status, all became topics that brands cared about as they navigated these new waters. As with all big lifestyle shifts, it drove them to want to know what the future householder would think, feel and do next – and my company was asked to forecast trends for companies who suddenly became interested in trend forecasting, from electricity providers to mattress brands and everything in between.

Of course, this is just a single snapshot of the change that led me to set up my own trend-forecasting agency. The change hasn't stopped, and if anything, the pace has quickened since then.

The rate of consumption and the pace of change we've experienced means that the level of responsibility placed on corporate decision makers has grown sub-stantially over the past twenty years. Senior leaders were once held accountable for the relatively simple goal of turning a profit, but today they are responsi-ble for driving much deeper and more transformative changes. Companies have experienced wave after wave of disruptive change that has put senior lead-ers under pressure to make quicker, better, safer deci-sions and deliver against the 'triple bottom line' – a term coined by John Elkington to describe the con-sideration of people, planet and profit. Leaders have turned to trend forecasting to help address these challenges.

Using trends to stay relevant

Staying relevant means being able to have a timely conversation with your customers. Businesses must perpetually be willing to change and adapt to meet their customers' social, cultural and ethical expec-tations to win their hearts and minds. Companies that change to remain relevant reap the rewards of being able to satisfy the evolving demands of their customers, because customers are emotionally and psychologically drawn to a brand that reflects their values and caters to their needs and desires.

Staying relevant means anticipating what will change for them, sometimes years in advance. People and societies are always changing their thinking – they never stand still. There is always a different angle or take on the world, and that can rapidly change the way an audience connects with a brand. However, it's not about asking your customers what they want. You must foresee shifts in the values, attitudes and behaviours that underpin all consumer lifestyle choices and inform what they will be drawn towards, long before they themselves know what that will be.

Whether you like it or not, shopping has become politicised, and the consumer infuses their purchasing choices with their ethics and values and scrutinises anyone they buy from. It's worth being mindful of the fact that, even if you consider your target customer *not* to be politically motivated, that doesn't much matter. The public scrutiny all companies come under now means that even small but vocal groups – who may never shop with you – possess a power that can draw attention to and boycott a global brand, and it can have rapid and devastating effects.

Audiences are savvy and well informed and bad news travels at speed thanks to social media. Consumers increasingly expect companies to be a positive force in shaping culture.[7] If companies fail to live up to expectations, shoppers will take their loyalty elsewhere. In the past, there was more margin for error and a company could make a mistake, course-correct and win customer loyalty back again, but now there is so much competition and so much choice, the customer will simply go elsewhere.

The connections the shopper makes between the product they buy from you and how relevant your brand is should not be underestimated. There is a ripple effect where a trend-driven product that resonates with a consumer can improve a company's reputation, and that can in turn drive greater market share. In other words, the empathy a brand shows to its customers creates a connection and drives loyalty.

In my career, I've often seen deep and profound reasons why trends matter to customers. These stretch way beyond a transactional product purchase. When a company executes trends well, they have the ability to make you feel like you belong, a point powerfully reinforced by journalist Frances Ryan. In her article for *The Guardian*, Frances shared her experience of growing up as a disabled child in the 1990s and says that although she saw all kinds of different dolls and figures, she never saw ones that represented

---

7   Edelman, 2024 *Edelman Trust Barometer Reveals Innovation Has Become a New Risk Factor for Trust* (2024), www.edelman.com/news-awards/2024-edelman-trust-barometer, accessed 9 April 2025

children with disabilities. She thought this lack of representation wasn't something toy companies seemed to consider. Ryan notes the impact of seeing yourself reflected in the world is subtle but powerful, shaping your sense of belonging.[8]

It is important, as a trend leader, that you ensure your business is not blind to these types of scenarios and that everyone understands the power of the products you sell and the impact they have. It's worth remembering the responsibility of producing any product or message that makes its way into society – and, whether you're being passive or intentional about it, it has real consequences.

The design application of trends may seem trivial, but the truth is that trends trickle all the way through an organisation, into the product that ends up in the hands of the customer. For example, you may be in charge of what phrase or motif gets printed on the side of a child's lunchbox. This is a lunchbox someone is going to buy for a child, which they will take to school every day for months, if not years. They are going to recognise it as their belonging and will remember what imagery and words are depicted on it. It's going to represent something about them – as

---

8   F Ryan, 'A rainbow playsuit and a pink ramp? Wheelchair Barbie is like looking in a mirror', *The Guardian* (27 December 2023), www. theguardian.com/commentisfree/2023/dec/27/rainbow-playsuit-pink-ramp-wheelchair-barbie-like-looking-in-a-mirror, accessed 9 April 2025

do all of our belongings. A signal to the world about who they are and what they like.

The world's best trend leaders are acutely aware of the impact they, in the product design world, have on the minds of customers. The trend leaders I've met get huge satisfaction from walking this line between driving commercial success and serving a customer who otherwise may not feel seen.

Conversely, when a company lacks relevance, it means that somewhere along the way, they have lost touch with what matters to their customer. The consequences of this are serious – and even some of the biggest brands and retailers have fallen victim to this.

We've seen what happens to brands that don't have a strong position on social justice issues or current affairs topics. At best, they are deemed to lack relevance with a modern consumer, and at worst, they get cancelled altogether. These brands have sometimes been in existence for many decades, but when a cultural reference point shifts, a brand can find itself wildly out of step.

Take for example the 130-year-old American syrup brand Aunt Jemima, the heritage of which came under scrutiny against the backdrop of renewed international debate about racism sparked by George Floyd's murder in 2020. The brand (whose imagery and name were based on a racial stereotype), experienced a backlash and, after 130 years, owners Quaker Oats were forced to retire it. Kristin Kroepfl, chief marketing officer at Quaker Foods North America, said in response, 'We must take a hard look at our portfolio of brands and ensure they reflect our values and meet customers' expectations.'[9]

Large corporations undoubtedly have the power to change things for better, but they are so often fixated on the aim of being as universally neutral as possible. We are moving towards a world in which that's just not possible or desirable. Brands that do well in the coming years will stand for something, with their values embedded into every part of their business.

Admittedly, it's relatively easy for a new, lean start-up company to bake ethics into the very foundations of its brand, manufacturing and strategy, but it's much harder to drive change through an organisation with thousands of product lines, millions of employees and billions of customers. However, herein lies the big opportunity for those who are bold enough to drive change.

There have been several societal shifts that impact the way consumers view brands. One such example is the rising awareness of how companies approach inequality, with attention on racial, economic, age,

---

9   B Kesslen, 'Aunt Jemima brand to change name, remove image that Quaker says is "based on a racial stereotype"', *NBC News* (17 June 2020), www.nbcnews.com/news/us-news/aunt-jemima-brand-will-change-name-remove-image-quaker-says-n1231260, accessed 12 May 2025

sexual orientation, religion, gender and disability inequality all receiving more scrutiny. Dr Jo Gooding is an inclusivity design researcher who advises organisations on how they can put inclusivity at the heart of their design and innovation process. She argues that a company that excludes and discriminates lacks relevance with the modern consumer. 'Brands who do not proactively build in inclusive design, risk launching a new product, process or idea that not only excludes a certain societal group, but that generates the wrong attention if it is deemed to be discriminatory,' she explains. 'The design of the world, its environments, products, and services, are often the barriers that make difference apparent. As designers and creators of these, brands have an important role in shaping and shifting entrenched norms.'[10]

Understanding future trends and what will shape them is the best way to maintain relevance. I can't think of a more compelling reason to use trend forecasting.

Accepting that change happens

If you're working for a company that isn't yet familiar with using trends, there is some groundwork to do around describing what trends are and how they'll make a difference.

---

10 Interview with Dr Jo Gooding conducted on 2 February 2024 for the purpose of this book

One of your first jobs when you are trying to initiate a future trend process is to build a baseline belief inside the organisation that forecasting trends is a business-critical activity. Like any new initiative, you'll need to put a business case together that demonstrates why understanding what your future customer will do next is so important. You'll need to persuade your colleagues that your current customer will behave differently in the future.

Before you do that, however, you'll need to prove that change happens. It sounds like an obvious thing to say, but to engineer the right mindset among your colleagues, you need to enable them to accept and agree that change does indeed happen.

One of the most effective techniques I use for demonstrating this is to show some case studies of other companies that anticipated change well, which helps build confidence inside an organisation and primes them for further conversations about future trends.

Reassuringly, you don't need to have a doctorate in foresight to be able to look around you and identify behaviours, lifestyles or products that are popular today that weren't popular two or ten years ago, or even just six months ago. Once you ask your colleagues to unpick the reasons why a current product or behaviour is popular, what led to its growth in popularity over time, and begin to retrospectively map out the signals and clues along the way that led to its success, you will be laying a cornerstone of acceptance with your colleagues that change does happen, and it will happen to your customers, too. If you're going to build a case for change, you need to remind people that trends are really, in their simplest form, expressions of change.

As a trend leader, you'll need to get your leadership team, peers and direct reports on board with the idea that trend forecasting is the best way to predict future change. You'll need to make a strong case – not just for the trends you believe you should adopt – but for why you think there's value in using trends in the first place.

At any given opportunity, make sure you knit together the act of trend forecasting with the language of staying relevant. Companies may not always understand why they need trend forecasting, but they will always appreciate the merits of staying relevant, and futures work is the key to demystifying what consumers will want next.

A note of caution – and I say this as someone who describes themself as a trend forecaster and founded a business with the word 'trend' in it: this word isn't always your friend. Sometimes, you need to swap it out with other words, such as change or relevance. Companies and individuals sometimes struggle with the word 'trend', especially if they are new to the world of trend forecasting. It can be misunderstood since it's a word that's entered our daily vocabulary and means different things to different people. Language really matters at the delicate early stages of introducing futures practices to an inexperienced business. However, 'relevance' is a word that's widely understood and something every brand wholeheartedly strives for.

When we ask our colleagues to accept that change happens, we also have a duty to share with them the consequences of inaction, too. The differentiator between a company that fails and one that succeeds has a lot to do with its readiness for change. Sometimes, this has nothing to do with what a company knows about future trends. In fact, I've seen global corporates with access to the best trend intelligence on the planet fail spectacularly, because having access to information isn't enough on its own – it's the ability to *act* upon the change they see coming that matters.

There are a number of reasons cited for the failure of toy retailer ToysRUs, when it collapsed back in 2017, but the two main reasons were its lack of innovation and its failure to adapt quickly enough to changing consumer behaviour. Undoubtedly this multibillion-dollar retailer invested heavily in understanding their future consumer, but they didn't respond in time.

So why are companies nervous about embracing change? Companies are operating in an environment where failure is costly; whether that's the financial and environmental cost of over-investing in a product that didn't sell and needs to be incinerated, or the cost of reputational damage from an audience backlash to a marketing campaign deemed controversial or inappropriate in some way. Today's volatile, uncertain, complex, ambiguous (VUCA) world means that markets are far more unstable, and that companies must adapt with flexible, forward-thinking strategies that anticipate change and mitigate risk.

This fear of failure has created a 'play it safe' mentality, and in the words of cultural theorist and author of ZINE, Matt Klein, 'We've lost sight of what it means to be brave. It feels like our facilities for riskiness and imagination have atrophied.'[11]

Companies might think it's better to play it safe by changing as little as possible, but the future consumer isn't interested in being served up sameness when their world is more dynamic than ever before. Personal value systems, culture, society, lifestyles, behaviours and tastes all change, and we expect the companies we buy from to keep pace. Many companies forecast too close to 'now' conditions, don't look far enough ahead (only decision making and forward planning on a quarterly basis) and aren't concerned enough with differentiating themselves.

---

11 M Klein, *The META Trending Trends: 02024* (Zine, 2024), https://zine. kleinkleinklein.com/p/meta-trends-2024, accessed 9 April 2025

When we forecast trends well, it should provide reassurance, robustness and confidence.

Reflection and action points

1. Evaluate how your company compares to the most progressive companies by using our Prepared for Change diagnostic tool, which will share a report on what you're doing well and where you have gaps. Just scan the QR code at the back of this book to access the tool.

2. Get familiar with your company's vision, mission and values, and diarise an annual touchpoint for an update on this as part of your internal calendar. Ask if there are any strategic goals or transformation projects the company is working towards, if it has an annual and longer-term strategic plan, and if it is working towards any future legislation you need to align with or inform.

3. Communicate to your business how staying relevant is dependent on having foresight of future social shifts. Show them stories of what happens when companies lack relevance and receive the wrong kind of attention.

4. Which trends has your company missed in recent years? Can you identify them? Can you categorise the trends they missed – for example, do they consistently miss technological shifts,

or fail to take notice when your customer does something different? Make a list of these as the starting point for building a case for using trends inside your company.

5. Talk about using trends for good. How might you ask your colleagues to reframe the challenges they see – in the business, or in society – and think about how they can create an opportunity to make life better?

TWO

What Makes A
Trend Leader?

I n this chapter, you will meet established trend leaders working inside large corporations and uncover
what motivates them to actively create a better future.

We will take a look at what makes a trend leader,
exploring the common characteristics across skills,
behaviours and education, and delve into the data
from research conducted especially for this book.

We will uncover why companies need to consider
having a trend leader, why we need to create more
of them just like you, and all of the career-enhancing
things that can happen when you fold trend leadership into your repertoire.

The role of a trend leader

A trend leader works to an extended time horizon and is responsible for building a picture of what will impact and influence their business in two to five years' time, or sometimes longer. Their job is to create the right environment where trends can be identified, discussed and adopted in an organised and timely manner.

Some people are intentionally hired into a trend role, but I regularly have conversations with those who have fallen into a trend leadership role out of necessity to meet a business need. Quite often, a head of design or marketing inadvertently acquires trend-leader status because they realise the business is stuck in some way. Perhaps a trend has hit their industry, yet their business has failed to act upon it, which prompts them to ask questions about what special insights their competitors may have had that their business didn't. In their effort to find a way for their business to look further ahead and spot the next set of challenges and opportunities, these professionals discover the futures industry and reach out to trend experts like me for help. They therefore become trend leaders simply because they find themselves responsible for hosting the conversation around trends on behalf of the entire business.

The trend leader's skillset enables them to become highly trusted individuals, who companies look to in order to get clarity on what's coming next and when the market will be ready to receive it. They are responsible for making multimillion-dollar consumer product decisions, ranging from selecting the next colour of the year for a paint company, to culturally critical decisions like how to avoid stereotyping when designing a doll. They must balance commercial success with brand reputation and find a way to innovate that ensures their business remains relevant to their audience.

You don't need to be a trend expert yourself to be a trend leader. Some of the greatest successes I've seen have come from people equipped at first with nothing more than a deep curiosity, a desire to help their company do better, and the courage to learn.

A trend leader is not there to research and forecast trends themselves, but they are responsible for managing the flow of trend information into the business and, critically, for *activating* the trends. Activating the trends means making sure ideas and information get translated into tangible outputs, like products or marketing campaigns, and this is work that is best done by someone inside of a company. While an external consultant or trend partner can gather a huge amount of trend intelligence and save you lots of time figuring out what the trends will be, it's you, as an internal company employee, who has the depth of knowledge that dictates how and when a trend is executed. As a trend leader, you play a pivotal role in advocating for a trend. Your job is to distil the essence of each trend into something that's perfectly right for the brand, and work with colleagues to ensure it gets applied across all appropriate areas of the business.

Typically, the role includes:

- Ensuring the business is looking sufficiently far enough ahead

- Fuelling the business with information so that it is informed about what change is coming and how this will generate opportunities and threats (which is usually achieved by commissioning trend intelligence from external providers, ensuring you have a good mix of information coming into the business)

- Forming a 'future picture' or narrative, so that their business can thrive rather than be a victim of the change that's inevitably coming (a large corporate business should have a detailed 'future picture' of the next three years to guide strategic decision making)

- Developing a culture of continually thinking about the future consumer and placing them at the heart of the business

- Making sure discussions about the future don't sit in silos in the boardroom or design department

- Creating good systems for sharing trend information

- Checking that trends are making it all the way through the business (from initial idea to product development) and are being actioned correctly

- Informing and unifying the key decision makers in the business

To be successful, trend leaders must have contact with multiple departments and teams throughout a business, from the board and senior leadership team to product design and marketing. Each of these departments benefit from using trends, but in my experience, it's the trend leader who must hold sole accountability for driving the process and directing the conversation around trends.

This idea is supported by a 2021 study by Dr Fabian Buder at the Nuremberg Institute for Market Decisions, who suggests that companies with a dedicated department and staff for strategic foresight generate more value for decision makers than companies that see foresight as a task for everyone.[12]

When I've seen this work well, trend leaders are perceived as conductors of the orchestra, knowing exactly which team members to invite into the ideation and decision-making process and when. The value that's created is huge when everyone understands what

---

12   F Buder, *The Value of Foresight in a VUCA World* (Nuremberg Institute for Market Decisions, 2021), www.nim.org/en/publications/detail/ research-report-the-value-of-foresight-in-a-vuca-world, accessed 12 May 2025

trends are, how they can drive growth and prevent costly mistakes, and how they can be used to reinforce decision making.

The career path to trend-leader status

I have met many formally trained internal foresight teams working inside billion-dollar brands, but I've seen just as many people succeed in the role of trend leadership with no formal training at all.

Today, there is more education available in the futures sphere than ever before – whether that is a post-grad qualification in strategic foresight, or a module in trend forecasting on a marketing degree – however, typically, a trend leader acquires their knowledge through self-directed learning while already in a corporate role.

In 2024, I conducted a LinkedIn poll of seventy-eight people of trend-leader status, which showed that 67% came from a design or product development career path, 15% came from market research, 10% came from a marketing route, and 8% described theirs as 'other' (which included coming from a purist trend forecasting background).

It is already a requirement of each of these disciplines of design, market research and marketing to be able to understand the customer you are serving, so it makes perfect sense that people working in these fields would be the ones best placed to be curious about what their customer will do next. I've seen design and marketing professionals strengthen their decision making by adding complementary future trends knowledge to their repertoire.

In fact, when we talk about what *makes* a trend leader, it's as much to do with the practical, hands-on experience they gain inside a corporation as it is about what or where they have previously studied.

MEET THE TREND LEADER

I first met Alex Post Miller when she was working at toy brand Mattel. Now a senior researcher in consumer insights at Netflix, Alex has a wealth of experience in applying trend research in a corporate brand setting.

'I didn't find trends, trends found me. I am so glad to have incorporated trends research into my repertoire as I do believe it has helped me in my career. It helps you think ahead, think strategically and think creatively, all of which are important leadership skills. It has helped me foster relationships internally and given creative autonomy to take risks.'[13]

Part of making a case for change means securing a budget for training and development for yourself and

---

13   Interview with Alex Post Miller conducted on 9 February 2024 for the purpose of this book

the team you build. Since we know that trend leaders are built and educated in the design, research and marketing departments, it means we know precisely where to invest to elevate and educate people into the role to bolster the business's chance of spotting changes on the horizon.

Scan the QR code at the back of this book for a list of resources, training, articles and podcasts to help you on your journey to trend leadership.

Leading positive change

My clients are trend leaders in some of the world's biggest companies and have been responsible for creating significant change. The results of their decisions ripple out and have the power to challenge societal norms, change attitudes, create new values, influence customers' emotions and shift their behaviours. One decision signed off by a trend leader can make the world a better – or worse – place. In a large corporate brand, you have the opportunity to put a trend into the hands of millions of customers and the capacity to be able to influence whole swathes of society. The compound impact of your decision making is huge.

Trends are a vehicle for companies to use products, imagery and language to shape the minds of their customers. Trends enable companies to alter an individual's self-perception and shift the lens through which they see themselves. Icons, motifs and slogans are an instant application of trends that have the power to encourage positive change in consumers, or conversely, to limit their mindset entirely.

It is for this reason that it really matters what words and graphics a designer puts on, say, a child's t-shirt. That language and imagery has the power to shape their sense of self. We mustn't trivialise the fact that if we exclusively and repeatedly tell girls they are princesses and boys they are ninjas, we become part of a system that limits their beliefs.

The trend leaders I've worked with are highly conscious of the responsibility bestowed upon them and are deeply committed to using trends to lead positive change and create a better future. It's a universal characteristic. I have seen trend leaders who use their influence to draw global attention to underrepresented and oppressed communities, and others who have passionately driven inclusivity for children in the toy industry. They have a deep-rooted desire to make a meaningful contribution and drive change in both the business they work in and in society more broadly, whether this is for the benefit of the teams that report to them, for their customers or for the planet.

Among the traits of a trend leader is the belief that companies can do better. They all feel the sense of responsibility to undo the damage that consumerism has caused over the decades (even if much of it happened before they entered the workplace). They have the desire and confidence to instigate change, not just passively respond to what's happening.

All of the trend leaders I've interviewed say they are working in alignment with their personal values and have a strong sense of purpose. They are clear about what matters to them and what they believe in, which is reflected in the broader market, too, as workers are increasingly drawn to working for companies that reflect their values. A 2022 study found that 61% of young employees said they chose their employer based on their values alignment.[14] Companies can expect employees to care about things like whether their employer is reliant on fossil fuels, or if they have a gender pay gap, or how inclusive the company's recruitment process is.

MEET THE TREND LEADER

The growing acceptance that trend forecasting is a business-critical activity is something that established trend expert Elisabetta Stacchiotti, Design Researcher and Strategist at Samsung Electronics has observed:

'I think that, as we notice that the world is in constant flux, there is a stronger need to be proactive and embrace change. In this scenario, trend tracking and forecasting are considered the smartest way to

---

14 Amba Good Work, *Amba Generation Gap Report* (Amba Good Work, 2022), www.amba-uk.com/resource/the-generation-gap-report, accessed 9 April 2025

anticipate future needs and remain relevant in the market – now, research isn't anymore a nice to have but a necessity, and this is probably the biggest shift I've observed in the last few years.

'When working in innovation, having strong ethics and a solid set of values focused on betterment, is fundamental to drive us toward taking the important choices.

'Big corporations have a real chance to influence and change the lives of many, so viewing decisions through the lens of higher values, such as sustainability and inclusivity, for instance, is simply a must.

'Everyone, in different business roles, has the option to choose where to stand and, as a trend researcher, I believe it is vital to strive to create a positive impact even in moments of crisis and uncertainty. Also, we shouldn't forget that consumers, especially Gen Y and Z, won't spend their money on unethical and unsustainable brands, so maybe, despite being slower than needed, even the corporate world is evolving in a more planet- and human-friendly way.'[15]

It's possible to work commercially and also have a strong sense of purpose. I've seen trend leaders walk the line between making high-stakes commercial decisions, and driving an ethical, societal and environmental agenda that allows them to stay true to their personal ethos of making the world a better place.

---

15 Interview with Elisabetta Stacchiotti conducted on 2 February 2024 for the purpose of this book

As a society, we are looking for exemplary leaders to help us move organisations and consumers through a period of dramatic and significant change, the likes of which have only been witnessed a handful of times before. The difference this time is that there is a pace to it: time is of the essence and the health of our planet depends on it.

We stand at the coalface of one of the most interesting, exciting and important points in industrial history, where audiences are asking brands to work to a higher purpose than simply putting products on a shelf.

This makes the job of a corporate trend leader both enviable and challenging. Enviable because their work can make a valuable impact all over the world, and challenging because they are required to have the answers and orient their company in a business landscape that's facing some of the biggest shifts – from geopolitical and societal to environmental and technological – in decades.

For those working in the futures industry, this is a challenge to be relished, as Alireza Hejazi, PhD, founding editor of peer-reviewed journal of leadership and futures studies *Nuts About Leadership* points out:

'It appears that futurists are impatient for the future to arrive. They are frustrated by how slowly things are changing. They want to go to the future as soon as possible. They want to detect it, shape it, forecast it, discuss it, live in it, envision it, share it, and make it a better place to live. They appear to be driven by curiosity, inspired by history, and enthralled by innovation, newness, and genuine ideas. They are eager to make the world a better place.'[16]

Characteristics of a trend leader

There are four stand-out characteristics or behavioural traits that unify trend leaders: imagination, diplomacy, appetite for evolution and persuasion. While these are by no means the only traits they exhibit, they are all innate traits in the trend leaders I've interviewed and met, and the ones that featured most prominently in a behavioural study conducted especially for this book.

Imagination

The dictionary definition of imagining is 'the action of forming new ideas, images or concepts of external objects not present to the senses'.[17] If forecasting future trends is about anything, it's about articulating things that are not present! Imagination plays a critical role in futures and foresight work, and yet it must

---

16   A Hejazi, 'Why does one become a futurist?', LinkedIn (3 July 2021), www.linkedin.com/pulse/why-does-one-become-futurist-alireza-hejazi-ph-d-/, accessed 12 May 2025

17   From the *Concise Oxford English Dictionary*

be delicately handled. The fruits of our imagination are often undervalued as being less reliable and more subjective than data and historical evidence, especially when we're using them to underpin million-pound decisions for large corporations.

The truth is, no one has the magical ability to truly *predict* the future, but imagining possible and plausible futures – and even creating a *preferred* future – is the job at hand. As trend leader, you'll not only have to get comfortable with the role that imagining the future plays, but you'll also need to persuade others of its importance and why it's not inferior to something backward-looking, like historic data:

> 'It's hard to imagine something until it's manifested in the physical. Imagine handing the iPhone that you're holding to someone 100 years ago; you'd probably be seen as a magical being of some sort, and who knows, you may even find yourself in danger for doing so. However, you're holding one now because someone imagined it, and look how normal it is. What we imagine, can be as real as what we hold in our hands. Imaginary is not nonexistent, it's more "we haven't seen it yet".'[18]

There is such power in the word 'yet' when it comes to future trends. If you're planning to work in the

---

18 P Thurston (n.d.) available at: www.instagram.com/thurstonphoto

business of seeing a future others can't yet see, the word 'yet' will be a real ally as you share ideas and forthcoming trends that might seem unfeasible – crazy, even – to your colleagues.

In a 2024 behavioural study that I conducted with Duo Global Consulting, 70% of trend leaders demonstrated their imagination by profiling heavily in visionary thinking, which means having a preference for the end vision and an ability to see the big-picture overview, being motivated to find new ways to do things, being flexible, considering multiple options and having a sense that possibilities are limitless.[19]

The study tells us that trend leaders:

- Prefer working in a more creative, unstructured way

- Have the ability to condense information into compelling overviews

- Appreciate the ability to have variety in their role

- See things with an 'unlimited possibilities' mindset

- Work better when able to work at a more visionary level

---

19 Duo Global Consulting, *Trend Leader Behavioural Study 2024* (Duo Global Consulting, 2024), commissioned by Joanna Feeley for the purpose of this book

- Prefer the bigger picture and a high-level view of things, rather than focusing on the details

Diplomacy

When discussions about trends get intense, a trend leader is there as 'host' to diffuse tension, to add context to contrasting views and to create an environment in which everyone's values are considered and views and opinions are shared respectfully.

Great trend leaders are highly regarded, and their contributions are valued – not because their business is any more receptive to change than another, or because their hit rate with trends is any more successful than the next person, but because they can control their emotions and tactfully manage their communications. They carefully guide colleagues through the ambiguity of dealing with the intangible future.

A credible trend leader needs to be visible in many layers of an organisation, be able to have peer-level conversations and have the respect of the executive team if they are to be influential. If you haven't already, as a trend leader, you will need to make peace with your role as an inspirer. You don't need to be the most charismatic or extroverted leader in order for people to believe in you. I've seen many effective trend leaders quietly and persistently making their voice heard.

One thing that strikes me as essential when I think of what's special about all the great trend leaders I've met, is not their skills, it is their demeanour. It is the ease and grace with which they conduct themselves. Their lack of ego or personal agenda means they instil a sense of confidence, and those around them have absolute faith in them. They are not opinionated egocentrics. While their personalities vary from person to person and business to business, their behaviours do not.

Appetite for evolution

Great trend leaders understand the risk associated with, and the power of, the new. Doing things differently and driving progressive change is something they naturally seek out. In the behavioural study mentioned earlier, 87% demonstrated an 'evolutionary change enthusiast' trait.[20]

Behavioural expert, Laura Weaving of Duo Global Consulting, who conducted the study, explains:

> 'One of the strong behavioural traits in trend leaders is their innate desire to progress ideas and drive change. This study measures how much respondents like things to remain the same, or whether, at the other end of the

---

20 Duo Global Consulting, *Trend Leader Behavioural Study 2024* (Duo Global Consulting, 2024), commissioned by Joanna Feeley for the purpose of this book

spectrum, they demonstrate a preference for radical change. 87% of trend leaders demonstrated the "evolution" behavioural pattern, which means they seek and are comfortable in a world of change.'[21]

What's interesting about these findings is that we know that people mostly come to trend leadership following a career in design, market research or marketing, so this desire to evolve and not stand still is deeply embedded in people's behaviours long before they consider working in trends. It's likely the reason why they find working with trends so appealing in the first place, along with the frustration they feel when they experience stagnation and see that change isn't happening in their company.

The study tells us that trend leaders:

- Like to constantly improve in how they do things

- Will almost always embrace change, if they can see the impact it will make

- Seek out ways to drive change in their work

- Will push the boundaries of change from time to time, and seek out more radical thinking that drives real innovation

---

21 Duo Global Consulting, *Trend Leader Behavioural Study 2024* (Duo Global Consulting, 2024), commissioned by Joanna Feeley for the purpose of this book

Persuasion

Some of the best trend leaders I've met are absolutely resolute about what kind of future agenda they are driving, and succeed in taking their colleagues on the journey with them because they have a gentle yet authoritative communication style. They can persuade time-poor senior executives, big-picture board members and in-the-detail designers with equal confidence.

If a trend they bring forth happens to feel too progressive for the business and creates a sense of nervousness, a great trend leader quietly and persistently makes their case again another time, all the while gathering more evidence and strengthening the rationale for the change. They advise, rather than urge, and are always careful to explain the potential consequences of ignoring or choosing not to act upon a trend they deem important. They persuade by blending their deep understanding of their customer with creativity and sound commercial decision making.

Being visible unlocks opportunity

In the previous chapter, we covered how trends enable companies and customers to prosper, but developing your understanding of trends will also help you personally progress your career – regardless of what level you're at. As a designer or product developer, you'll always be more employable if you're able to work with trends, and you will be able to unlock opportunities and create a position for yourself that benefits the business and raises your professional profile. At a senior level, trend leadership gives those from a design or marketing background the opportunity to elevate themselves to board level, bringing a valuable skillset that isn't typically demonstrated by others around the board table who may have come from a financial, operations or commercial background.

Having the ability to articulate a future that others can't yet see – and then convince them of its validity – is a really distinctive skillset and makes you more visible inside an organisation. Someone who can see future opportunities and outline emerging risks really stands out and becomes an indispensable employee. Executive teams and boards are keen to have people who can help them anticipate what lies ahead and plan accordingly. When you become associated with developing the path forward for a business, you become known as *the* person who thinks about the future. You'll draw other forward thinkers to you and unlock the most interesting and exciting career opportunities.

At the start of my own career as a fashion designer, I worked for American Eagle Outfitters in New York, which grew explosively in a short space of time, and found itself struggling to keep up with customer demand. The design team around me were working hard to meet the demands of an expanding list of store openings and product lines. I spotted an opportunity to support the designers with trend information to help them identify what was coming next in terms of styles, colours, motifs and graphics. I asked my boss if I could take responsibility for working on trends in addition to my day job as design assistant, and he agreed that it sounded like a good way to fuel the design team with new ideas. My visibility in the company went from glorified intern status to valued employee, and it unlocked conversations with the design directors, heads of buying and the executive team who all were suddenly more interested in what I had to say. It was the first step for me towards my trend-forecasting career, and, even better, it was an opportunity I had unlocked for myself. I progressed from that job a few years later into several roles where I was hired *because* of my trend-forecasting skillset.

Later, I held the role of trend leader for several large retailers and brands. I remember how exhilarating it was to identify the seed of a new idea, convince the business to invest in it, see the press get excited about its launch, and watch the consumer demand for it grow. My ability to spot opportunities to serve unmet needs soon drew attention and accelerated my career.

On the flip side, I also experienced what it was like when trends weren't followed, when competitor companies enjoyed huge success after following a trend we had failed to act on, and I recall being the one personally called into the CEO's office to unravel the design process and understand why, knowing that this meant someone's job might be on the line. I know only too well the type of pressure that exists in every decision taken by trend leaders.

Over time, you get to drive change inside the organisation and become known as someone who helps the business face its biggest challenges. Being visible unlocks opportunities to network widely, to be part of important conversations, to get promoted, to lead on projects and even to be the external face of the business.

Even in a business that doesn't have a traditional product development structure, individuals who are switched on to change can drive interesting and beneficial initiatives and can create a strong profile for themselves while doing so. In these businesses, I see emerging trend leaders, driven by their innate sense of curiosity, start to ask questions like, 'Who is looking to the future in this company? In what way can we say we're prepared?'

MEET THE TREND LEADER

One such person is Ruby Sommer, Creative Manager at utility company Northumbrian Water Group, who took exactly this approach, allowing her to go from graphic designer to creative manager. She now commissions future trend reports to help the company understand its consumers and better anticipate unmet needs:

'Decision making in utility companies historically relies on hard data, but NWG is well known for thinking outside the box with things like our annual innovation festival. It has provided solutions for many problems facing the water sector, like inventing a rural sensor to reduce the time to report water leaks by half and developing an app to track and reduce householder energy and water consumption.

'Because it's typically such a data-driven industry, in the past it was challenging to present new ideas. Using trend forecasting to set the future context has been invaluable, and has helped me to increase my visibility, and build and use my personal influence. It has heavily supported buy-in to new concepts and ideas. Sharing the science behind trend forecasting has enabled me to have credibility when presenting my ideas and has also led to me being asked to contribute towards a variety of projects where there are questions around future fit for purpose.'[22]

Reflection and action points

1. To be successful, businesses need someone looking at the future at all times.

2. Knowing what the trends are is only half the job – knowing what to do with them and keeping them alive in your business is where the work is, and it is best done by people who already work inside your business.

---

22 Interview with Ruby Sommer conducted on 31 January 2024 for the purpose of this book

3. You can use trends to improve your visibility and career status.

4. What kind of trend leader are you right now? Do you know which areas you need to develop? Now is a great time to take our diagnostic test to evaluate which skills you have already, and which areas you need to focus on next. The test can be found by scanning the QR provided at the end of this book.

5. Don't be afraid to position yourself as a trend leader.

6. Identify a senior leadership champion who can amplify your voice in the right groups.

PART TWO

INTRODUCING THE SIX GUIDING PRINCIPLES FOR TREND LEADERSHIP

THREE

Principle One: Create A Trend Framework

This chapter explores the first of my guiding principles of trend leadership,: creating a trend framework.

One thing I've found that allows the world's best brands to stand out is that they have a strong internal process. When I work with a company that has not used trends before, it's the first thing I put in place.

In this chapter, I'll share some of the foundational activities you can include to help create a reliable framework for introducing trends to your business.

This chapter will help you find out what information already exists inside the business by conducting a trend audit, create a cyclical roadmap that brings structure and clarity, and create a compelling kick-off event to inspire your stakeholders. I'll show you how to keep your concepts and trends intact as they make their way through the whole product development cycle by understanding what erodes and impedes them.

Conduct a trend audit

Before you look to bring in any trend forecasting, it's a good idea to find out what information is used by the business and measure how trends currently perform.

There are two trend audits I recommend conducting: a trend resource audit and a trend performance audit.

Trend resource audit

A trend resource audit is an investigation into what trend intelligence a business has, where it can be located and who is using it. Information can sit in various silos across a large organisation and can be hard to access. A comprehensive audit is a useful starting point for you to see where you might need additional support, and where there may be duplication of resources.

The purpose of conducting a trend resource audit is so that you can feel sure that you are accessing reputable, timely trend intelligence that will keep your company informed about change. The risk of not having the right intelligence in your business is that you miss a trend, which could be anything from a lifestyle shift that was indicated in a demographic study, to a colour trend that was predicted in a colour forecast.

A trend resource audit will help you:

- Know where the business is currently getting its trend intelligence from (if it is getting any!)

- Measure efficiency – noting duplications, or unused trend resources – providing the opportunity to consolidate and save costs

- Determine the volume and location of trend resources – which divisions are switched on to thinking about and researching the future?

- Understand the accessibility of trend resources across departments

- Measure the level of current investment in resourcing future trends

- Identify gaps in knowledge that may exist – are you routinely missing trends in a specific area because it is under resourced?

So, what classifies as trend intelligence?

In most large companies, there is customer, product and market intelligence, in various pockets all over the organisation. Trend intelligence includes reports, data, presentations, keynotes, conferences and sub-scriptions – you can scan the QR code at the back of this book to download a list of resource examples. You may learn that the finance team subscribe to reports that help them anticipate market conditions, or that the market research team buy in demographic stud-ies, or that the design team attend trade shows each year.

Some trend leaders I have worked with have a central-ised online hub through which people can access the company's full suite of futures and trend information. An audit is not about gatekeeping information – you don't necessarily want to prevent other colleagues or divisions from consuming their own trend informa-tion – but it is about ensuring you're fully informed.

It's abundantly clear when different divisions inside an organisation are working from their own set of futures resources and there is no joined-up think-ing. For example, many years ago, I worked with a global coffee company that was looking to rejuvenate their brand and dominate the in-home instant cof-fee market. Their senior leadership team had been busy buying trend reports about the behaviours of Generation X, and the marketing team had been focusing on Millennials. Each department was mak-ing a different set of assumptions that were leading them to build different pictures of who their customer was and what their needs were. Months of hard work and their entire brand positioning project was at risk because it was confused and had been attracting two different audiences who were at different life stages. Thankfully, we uncovered this at an early stage, but there have been brands who have gone to market with conflicting product and marketing messages that tell completely different stories, simply because they had been leaning on different sets of trend information.

It isn't just about what information exists, but how each team uses it that you need to track. Which teams are working the furthest ahead? Is everyone working to the same rhythm – seasonal or annual, for example? Are different divisions working to different time horizons – for example, is the board working to understand the commercial trading landscape over the next five years, while a designer is trying to understand colour trends for the next twelve months? It's natural that different divisions will use different types of futures intelligence, but as trend leader, you will need to have knowledge of what's happening across the business.

Conducting a trend resource audit shouldn't be a one-off event either, and it's a good idea to update your records every year, as Alex Post Miller of Netflix explained when I interviewed her:

> 'It is often about determining who has access to what trends and from where. Sometimes that means consolidating vendors or analysing and looking across to find additional patterns.

In both instances the goal is to remove redundancies and validate trends.'[23]

Conducting a trend resource audit is a good opportunity to raise your visibility and to help colleagues see what futures intelligence is already feeding into the company.

Trend performance audit

How good is your company's track record for responding to trends?

Poor past or current performance is often why a company with no experience of working with trends reaches out to me. Sometimes, a business has missed a trend, or it's difficult to get the business to understand that trend forecasting could be the solution to better understanding the future consumer.

Is there a particular area you think you fall down as a business? Can you identify if this is strategic, or if your product is missing something or that the trend doesn't land at the right time for your audience? I often speak with trend leaders who express frustration that a competitor is onto a trend six months or a year before them and they feel this hinders their opportunity to be seen as market-leading, meaning they miss the best press coverage opportunities.

---

23 Interview with Alex Post Miller conducted on 9 February 2024 for the purpose of this book

Clearly, conducting a performance audit has to be researched and delivered with sensitivity (you may have colleagues who were responsible for instigating a trend that didn't do well, for example) but when done well, it can be truly enlightening.

Can you evidence three to five trends you think you've missed or you were too slow (or too quick) to respond to, and compare that with what your competitors produced in response to the same trends? Can you equate the size of the opportunity and list the benefits that this afforded to your competitors? This is important information about trend performance that you can share with your stakeholders.

We'll talk more about the importance of tracking trends later on, in Chapter Seven, but the more informed you are when it comes to how trends perform for your business, the more credibility you will build, and the more people will look to you as the key person of influence when it comes to trends.

Performance is always a hot topic for those in your executive team, who will be better persuaded when you can show them historical evidence of how past trends have worked or the opportunities that competitors have capitalised upon. Building this picture of how trends currently perform in your business will form an important justification trail of supporting data that will build their confidence in working with trends.

Create a trend roadmap

A trend roadmap is a planning tool – a timeline or schedule of activity – designed to help your business identify and nurture trends and ensure momentum isn't lost through the product development, manufacturing and marketing process.

A trend roadmap can include:

- A research and analysis phase – discovering what trends are coming and analysing whether and how they will impact your business and future customer

- An ideation phase – inviting discussion and coming up with ideas that respond to the trends you think are most important

- A kick-off event to officially launch the new cycle or season and involve key stakeholders

- Sign-offs, selections or approvals by stakeholders who are checking new ideas for commercial or brand fit

- The design process

- Sampling and sample reviews

- Tracking and monitoring the impact or performance of the product when it hits the market – this can be press coverage, sales, market share etc

As the person responsible for hosting the conversation around trends, a roadmap can help you plot progress and answer questions about why you are (or are not) responding to a trend as a business, where in the development pipeline a trend is and when your customer can expect to feel the benefit. The idea of having a structured approach is that it creates a calmer, more organised working environment. As you start out in your role as trend leader, you'll likely be juggling more than the responsibility for how the company spots and executes trends, so you need this particular part of your job to run as smoothly as possible.

As well as the trend roadmap being a tool that's personally useful for you, it's also incredibly important for your stakeholders. Having a trend roadmap in place communicates to all stakeholders that bringing a trend to life is a *process* with a tangible outcome that is measured on a timeline. In businesses that are new to working with trends, there can be a lot of mystery and misinterpretation as to how trends get crafted and rolled out, so having this formalised timeline and structure unifies your colleagues and gives clarity.

Harnessing constant change

Change is happening all the time and although you will not act upon every single trend that's coming, you need to be aware of the important shifts that will impact your future customer.

Although we can accept that change is constant, we must also accept that your time, and your company's timescales, are finite. Therefore, we have to respond to the change that's happening in a structured way. New ideas and trends can spring up at any time, but your trend roadmap will make it clear that there is a specific window in your process where you'll be able to accommodate and activate them. The sweet spot is striking a balance between being open to and aware of change, being agile enough to respond to it, and running an organised and productive business.

Spotting trends isn't an ad hoc activity. When I interviewed him in 2024, Herb Kim, founder of TEDx Newcastle and Thinking Digital Conference, explained that, 'Looking at trends in an ad hoc way is like aiming a cannon, once, in one direction, and expecting to hit your target.'[24]

It surprises me how many large companies treat trend forecasting as a one-off activity. When trend forecasting is not properly embedded, I see companies doing standalone activities such as inviting an expert to come into the business to talk about a current subject, or inconsistent activities like commissioning a trend forecast one year but not the next. Great companies know they need to be consistently well informed and that there must be a rhythm to their process for spotting trends and responding to them. This requires a

---

24 Interview with Herb Kim conducted on 7 February 2024 for the purpose of this book

trend roadmap, a visual journey that can be used by all stakeholders, key contributors and collaborators and which maps the trend from concept to its realisation within your company.

It's common that companies new to the trend-forecasting process underestimate how far ahead they need to be working. Often a company has an established design or product development process in place, but nowhere near enough time set aside to understand future trends.

Each industry works to its own cycle, so timings will differ depending on whether you make a tangible product or not, and how long it takes to get that product to market. If you're a kitchen cabinet manufacturer, you might work to a five-year product development cycle, if you make greetings cards, you may create new collections every six weeks. Some product development, like paint, baby food or laundry detergent, requires complex chemistry, rigorous testing, new legislation or new technologies to launch a new idea safely, so it takes years to get a product to market.

If you launch new products once every five years, that does not mean you should only research fresh trends once every five years. A lot can change in a five-year period, and a truly resilient company will be open to regularly hearing about what's changing for the future consumer.

As a trend leader you will be heavily involved in the front end of the innovation and design process, but to be successful you need to maintain your involvement at specific touchpoints throughout the product development process. The final output (which may or may not be a tangible product, it could be a behaviour you're looking to shift or a marketing campaign) must stay as true to your vision as possible, which involves staying connected to how the trend is unfolding in your business but without providing constant supervision. Having a trend roadmap helps you plot your involvement, embed the process and set expectations among colleagues. Engineering these key moments that are dedicated to identifying and discussing trends into your development cycle will not only help create an organised framework, but they will also become an integral part of the company's culture.

Working to multiple time horizons

It's important to have a strong handle on your company's product development cycle and launch dates, and then consider what type of activities need to happen before that in your trend roadmap.

Working sufficiently far ahead means you will have to embrace overlapping cycles and different time horizons. By this, I mean you may be in the ideation phase for a product collection that gets launched in two years' time, and you may simultaneously be working on the marketing campaign for a different product collection that is ready to go and gets launched in three months' time. Many companies shrink down their trend-forecasting process simply because they only want to work on one product development cycle at a time. If you can develop a tolerance for overlap, the business will be all the more robust for it.

It can feel overwhelming to work simultaneously to multiple time horizons. It requires a framework with clear steps that holds you steady so that you know where you are in your process.

To create your own trend roadmap, choose a format that meets your needs – it can be a Gantt chart, a timeline or something more visual. For a sample Trend Roadmap, you can access a template in the free resources that come with this book by scanning the QR code at the back of this book.

Host a kick-off

A kick-off is an event that marks the beginning of a new trend cycle. It can be a workshop, facilitated discussion or a trend presentation. It's a way to share material to prompt fresh thinking and discussion and encourage teams to collaborate, hear different views and be reminded that change happens. The important thing here is that a kick-off marks the point when everyone gathers to think about the future of the business. It is a great way to enthuse and inspire your colleagues and many people say their trend kick-off event is their favourite work event of the year.

So, what might a kick-off look like? It depends on how familiar your company is with using trends, and your kick-offs can evolve over time as your colleagues become more familiar with using trends. For example, I hosted a fifty-person workshop for a design team who knew little about how trends worked. To build their understanding of the trend-forecasting process, I split them into groups of five and gave each group a product to analyse that was popular at the time, and asked them to work together to unpick the rationale for how that product got to be so popular. I asked them to work backwards and unravel the behaviours and needs of the consumer that led to this product being so desirable. I asked them to think about how the product was made – did some new innovation need to occur for this product to become a reality? Perhaps a new material or a new manufacturing pro-cess? I asked them to identify which lifestyle trends underpinned the desire for this product – what feel-ing or emotion was the customer seeking when they bought it? The groups were able to rewind the journey of the product, articulate which trends prompted it and see its origins, which helped reinforce their belief in the trend-forecasting process.

A team more experienced in using future trends may be able to listen to a trend presentation and contribute to an ideation session to discuss how a forthcoming trend might apply to their division or category.

Perhaps your kick-off might be a trend conference where you invite colleagues, a trend agency or other speakers to come and provide fresh thinking and get everyone up to speed with what's changed. Or it might be a brainstorming session with your team using a digital brainstorming app like Miro, where you can gather everyone's research and ideas in one place.

In the words of futurist Caitlin Keeley, 'the future belongs to those who think about it'.[25] A kick-off is all about creating space to think about the future.

Think about:

- Who to *invite* and who to *inform* – not everyone needs to be at the kick-off, and colleagues who are not there can still stay connected to your process without inviting them to join the discussion

- How to use your kick-off as a way to create a buzz inside the business and link this to your mission of having a better understanding of the future consumer

- Where you'll host it and the experience you'll wrap around it to generate the best engagement

The purpose of your kick-off is to inspire and engage. You will lean on the goodwill created in your kick-off

---

25   https://caitlinkeeley.com

at other points in your development process when you need your colleagues in design and marketing to do the hard work of activating the trends. Over time, you'll notice your colleagues becoming more comfortable with thinking about the future, enthusiastically imagining what the future might look like. The more engaged they are at this stage, the more you'll be able to persuade them to pay attention to important trends, and develop their trend knowledge.

You can build interest and excitement around your kick-off by creating a special invite for your colleagues or issuing some juicy soundbites in a newsletter or video to get them to think about topics before the event itself. This is a great opportunity for you to take ownership for hosting the kick-off, and is a great place to build your own profile.

WATCH OUT

A note of caution: while it's common for companies to host a 'trend day' or innovation day where they welcome external speakers, it's dangerous to assume a single day of inspiration will do the job of keeping a company safe from the winds of change. It's not to say it won't have *any* impact, but it's a lot of pressure to put on a single event. Hearing about tomorrow's big-picture topics will inspire your team, but if it's too abstract, it won't get actioned. To *inspire action* is to take the extra steps to apply the trends to your industry and business challenges.

The goal of a kick-off is to instil ownership and inspire people to *act*. The best brands I've worked with go beyond a single event and craft a whole programme for responding to change, which they articulate through their trend roadmap.

How to avoid concept erosion

Strange things can happen to a new idea as it travels through a business. Since a new idea or trend must make its way through several teams in different departments, each with their own agendas, opinions and objectives, it needs to be tracked to avoid concept erosion. This is when you start out with a defined idea, but as it goes through the product development journey, the trend gets chipped away at until it bears no relation to the original concept.

There's nothing more demoralising for a trend leader than meticulously researching and validating their trends over weeks or months, producing trend materials and delivering a kick-off event, only for faith in it to dwindle as it limps through the design and sampling process and eventually stalls. Of course, not every trend and idea *should* make it all the way through the process; there are good reasons why trends sometimes get shelved, but as trend leader, it's important you know why this is.

For example, a designer working in upholstered furniture may spot an opportunity to use a new material, such as mycelium (a type of sustainable mushroom protein being used as a leather alternative), but this gets parked at the sampling phase because it's too difficult to find manufacturers who will work with it at scale. Because it becomes difficult to produce, it gets swapped out for something that is a poor substitute – like polyester, that doesn't have the sustainability credentials, and the whole concept becomes completely eroded.

Dilution and oversimplification

Concept erosion can also come in the form of a dilution or oversimplification of a theme or story that loses its power and richness as it becomes adopted. For example, around 2016, the Danish cultural concept and feeling of *hygge* became a popular lifestyle trend that spread throughout Europe and the USA, inspired by the much-coveted levels of Danish happiness and contentment. At the height of this trend, over 500 book titles were published on the subject (interestingly, none of them were published in Denmark), and retailers made millions exporting and commercialising this as a cosy décor concept.

With Denmark consistently ranked among the top countries in The World Happiness Report (an annual publication that ranks countries based on the happiness of its citizens), it's easy to see why its culture and lifestyle would be a source of such fascination at a time when the rest of the world was reporting rising levels of over-working, poverty and an epidemic of loneliness.[26] Hygge became attractive because it appeared to exemplify – and chimed with – a growing global focus on improving wellbeing. It's quite possible that Danes cherish hygge precisely because it cushions them against their own set of hardships; namely their long, cold, dark, isolating winters.

Although there are hygge activities and lifestyle elements to this trend that promote feelings of contentment and cosiness – characterised by soft lighting, cosy blankets and candles – the origins and meaning of hygge run much deeper than that and it cannot be reduced to a series of cosy objects and activities. Denmark's culture, politics and social democratic system provide a particular lifestyle built on equality and a strong welfare system that has the necessary foundations for a culture of equality, simplicity and finding joy, and that enables its people to focus on and create an atmosphere conducive to enjoying the simple pleasures promised by hygge. There was a craving for the deeper meaning of hygge in places like the UK and USA, but the meaning of the concept was distilled into a few objects, when at a deeper level, it could have prompted a more transformative conversation about our lifestyle choices.

---

26 Wellbeing Research Centre, *World Happiness Report 2025* (University of Oxford, 2025), https://worldhappiness.report, accessed 9 April 2025

This is perfectly summarised by Danish resident, podcaster and comedian Abby Wambaugh in the Help Hole podcast episode, 'The Little Book of Hygge':

> 'It feels like it's buying into the idea that you can just have this feeling if you do a puzzle by candlelight. There is a component that's like, yes, a puzzle by candlelight is like the hyggelig feeling. However, underneath that, the people doing the puzzle by candlelight only worked thirty-six hours this week, have five weeks of vacation a year, have never paid for braces for their children, and have fifty-two weeks, paid parental leave. There's an underlying base of safety that makes that feeling possible.
>
> 'It's really hard to sit and do a puzzle if you're afraid you can't pay your rent and you have three jobs and you're on the phone in the queue to the NHS to try and get life affirming care and it's not happening.'[27]

So concept erosion can surface from a whole range of decisions, the consequences of which are both big and small. In order that you notice the way a trend is being interpreted, shaped and skewed by decisions along the way, you'll need to have regular contact points throughout your process. Does the end result

---

27   A Wambaugh, 'Episode 9: Help Hole', The Little Book of Hygge (2024), https://podcasts.apple.com/gb/podcast/help-hole-with-sofie-hagen-and-abby-wambaugh/id1725293250?i=1000653884579, accessed 9 April 2025

look like you imagined it would? Have cost restrictions impaired or ruined the product to the point that it no longer reflects the trend the future consumer is looking for?

Create check-in points along your trend roadmap to see how the trends are developing, and be prepared to have conversations about course-correcting them back to their original values to avoid trends being poorly or incorrectly interpreted.

Schedule activation sessions

Each company's product development cycle varies, but there are a number of touchpoints you need to put in place if an idea is going to make it intact from the conceptualisation stage and into your customers' hands.

After the sharing of trend intelligence in your kick-off, you need to move quite quickly to the next phase, which must include some kind of process for ordering the information and for selecting which trends you will apply.

Your roadmap needs to include a number of activation points. This is a series of check-ins and consultations with your colleagues to make sure that the trends you have identified as important in your kick-off are still alive and being interpreted authentically. It's also an opportunity to spot any concept erosion.

In this section, I will show you how to get the most from your activation sessions.

Do not underestimate the importance of hosting activation sessions. It's simply not enough to host an inspirational trend kick-off and then let your design and marketing teams just go off and independently select, interpret and apply them. Having a trend leader who can work on the details with these teams in smaller groups is where much of the hard work is done.

MEET THE TREND LEADER

When I interviewed her, Elisabetta Stacchiotti, Design Researcher and Strategist at Samsung Electronics, agreed:

'There are many qualities that a good trend forecaster should have, like empathy, intuition and analytical thinking but I believe that a trend leader's most important quality is the ability to interpret a trend and envision an activation strategy specific to their brand or company to provide real opportunities for innovation.'

Spotting important forthcoming trends is certainly a critical part of the trend leader's skillset, but 80% of my clients at TrendBible tell me their biggest challenge is activating trends. This means they can have a high awareness of an emerging customer attitude or behaviour, but they struggle to bring their response to fruition.

I recommend three types of interactions to help you translate ideas and insights into evidencable outputs, such as products and marketing campaigns. They are selection meetings, status reports and consultations.

Selection meetings

Trends and new ideas need to be purposefully committed to, and your company will need to boldly articulate which trends you are and are not responding to. As soon as you begin to introduce trends to your business, you'll realise that someone must be accountable for agreeing which trends you will and won't respond to. There are a number of ways that trend selections are made, from democratic approaches in which everyone gets a vote, to nominating small sign-off committees, or more autocratic decision making where one person makes the selection. In some companies, the role falls to the trend leader, the head of design, the CEO or even a shareholding family member if it's a family business. One thing is for certain: there is *always* a reason why a trend does or doesn't get selected – the person or group selecting the trends must work hard to articulate their rationale and avoid woolly reasons such as 'gut feelings'. The more your team know about the ingredients that make a great product or idea the better.

It may be that your first step is forming a sign-off committee who are responsible for ranking and selecting trends. You may need to make a compelling business case for why certain committee members need to be included to ensure you get a good balance of views that work in the business's *and* the future consumer's best interests.

To get the most from your selection meetings, make sure you are scoring each trend against:

- Importance – rate each of the trends or ideas out of ten – which are the ones you simply *must* act upon and why?

- Urgency – at what point will this trend or idea be most relevant for your customer?

- Feasibility – is this trend doable given your resources?

- Brand fit – how aligned is this trend with your 'house style', your vision, values and category specialism?

As trend leader, it's possible that you won't get final sign off on which trends the company goes ahead with. However, it is important for you to host the conversation, to provide clear frameworks for gathering the selection committee's criteria, and that you explain what the cost of not pursuing a trend would be. (See the free resources that come with this book for a Trend Selection Scorecard template you can use to keep track of how you have ranked and selected your trends.)

Status reports

Creating a status report for trends is critical so that you can keep your colleagues informed on progress at any given moment in the product development cycle. A status report enables the whole business to see the journey of the trend as it makes its way through your business and comes to life. This can include a series of check-ins with design, buying, merchandising and marketing team members, who can present progress back to you using designs and samples.

If you're working on a physical product, it's always worth taking photos at each touchpoint through the journey, too. This sometimes illuminates a specific point in your product development process where things get changed beyond all recognition, so it helps you build a case for how you'll navigate your next product when it hits this same point in the process.

Consultations

Engineer a role for yourself as trend leader so that, throughout the product development process, designers and other colleagues know they can come to you for advice and guidance and to discuss the trends.

It's important you communicate to the business that your involvement doesn't just belong at the 'front end' of product development; you'll be there to guide them throughout the process. You can do this by launching a series of ninety-minute consultations at key moments in your product development process – say, for example, the three-month, six-month and nine-month points. During these consultations, you can use tools such as a SWOT analysis to evaluate specific designs, and cross-reference samples and designs against the rationale that was given in the trend selection document. If your company covers different product areas – for example, if you produce a textile bedding collection and a ceramic decorative accessories collection – it's a good idea to bring together teams from the different departments involved. This way, everyone will understand how their decisions affect the bigger picture and can work together to create a more cohesive and well-curated final result.

Reflection and action points

1. Conduct an audit – what future trend resources do you have available to the business currently and are there any information gaps? What's your track record as a business for responding to trends – where do you get it right and wrong?

2. Host a seasonal or annual kick-off – a trend seminar or workshop to signal the start of the innovation process. Send an invitation to your colleagues to generate excitement – the more engaged they are, the stronger their commitment to executing the trends will be.

Use the opportunity to become more visible as the host for conversations about the future. Don't be afraid to take small steps at first. Your kick-off can even be an event that tells your colleagues what trends are and why they matter in the first place, leaning on what you uncovered in your trend audit.

3. Create a trend roadmap diarising the key touchpoints of the whole process, from research gathering, to concept ideation, to design, sampling and testing.

4. Be clear about where your development cycles may overlap and explain that different teams may be working to different time horizons, which is necessary for you to work sufficiently far enough ahead as a business.

5. Create a visual log of the products that are being developed.

6. Set up trend consultations that your colleagues can book at key moments in your product development process so they can benefit from your advice and guidance.

FOUR

Principle Two: Hold Space For Curiosity And Challenge

Fostering a culture of curiosity and challenge is crucial for being able to identify and embrace emerging trends. Building an environment in which colleagues feel comfortable raising questions and exploring new ideas – even those that are radical or uncomfortable – helps generate creative solutions, inspires innovation and develops a sense of collective exploration.

In a progressive company, new trends are identified, nurtured and brought to life, robustly interrogated for brand fit, and seen from a variety of perspectives to give them the best chance of success. It's important to create a culture in which it's safe to explore and articulate new ideas – and also to challenge them.

Trend leaders never work alone, and part of their job is to create space for discussion and debate about trends inside the business. A trend leader is a conduit through which an abundance of insight and intelligence flows. They act as a hub for information and insights. They balance influencing and inspiring others with listening and understanding, knowing that getting stakeholders on board with a new trend is critical to its success.

A good trend leader is able to connect with colleagues at all levels and across multiple departments. The first challenge of being able to get a trend into the hands of the customer is an internal one. This means helping it to make its way from an ambiguous concept to a clear idea that's fully embraced by the company – from the board to the design team, merchandisers, buyers, suppliers and marketers.

It is the trend leader's job to clearly communicate where and when in the process colleagues are permitted or expected to contribute.

In this chapter, we'll explore how to engage stakeholders and how to involve them in trend conversations, how to foster divergent thinking, embrace opposing viewpoints and scepticism, and navigate healthy conflict.

Foster a culture of curiosity

Cultivating a working environment that champions curiosity is a great way to surface trends and get buy-in from your colleagues at an early stage in the trend process.

Curiosity fuels creative and imaginative thinking, which are critical for encouraging your team to look beyond the present. In businesses that value curiosity, I see teams actively spending time researching, thinking about, imagining and discussing trends, and asking good questions to uncover insights and unlock possibilities. A company that encourages its people to engage with new trends and welcomes their participation is a great environment for trends to thrive.

The best trend leaders schedule touchpoints in their trend roadmap to involve their colleagues, with the aim of stimulating new ideas and creating a conversation about what's changing and why.

When you foster curiosity, it encourages your team to seek new knowledge, develop a questioning attitude, explore deeper insights and broaden their perspectives. It also helps you as trend leader to get a balanced read on how your colleagues feel about any trends you are proposing and avoid any pushback coming too late in the process for you to respond.

Part of the spirit of keeping a trend alive in the business is to build a culture in which you're collectively and continually asking, 'What's changing for our audience?' If you can stay close to that question, you'll be heading in the right direction.

So, what does a culture of curiosity look like in practice? It means that every team member feels empowered to raise questions, to challenge assumptions and to contribute to discussions about future trends. This level of engagement often involves dedicated training, equipping individuals with the skills to communicate thoughtfully and engage in respectful debate.

Activities like brainstorming sessions are useful where you can invite colleagues to digest new information and talk about a trend's pros and cons. You can create opportunities for open dialogue by using apps such as Slack, where you can add a running commentary and discussion board for each trend.

Discussions about trends are different to other types of conversations we might have in a business. Future trends are often intangible, lacking concrete data points to support early observations. As a result, individuals may feel a sense of vulnerability when sharing their insights or challenging established ideas. It is within this context that a company culture that embraces mistakes as learning opportunities becomes paramount. When failure is viewed as a stepping stone to innovation, teams are more likely to embrace the uncertainty inherent in trend forecasting, leading to more robust and insightful predictions.

A culture of curiosity thrives when:

- There are moments in the trend roadmap for stakeholders to familiarise themselves with future trends

- People can freely ask challenging questions about potential future trends

- There is a continuous, collective effort to understand the evolving needs and desires of the target audience

- People feel that their ideas are being heard but also understand that there is process beyond the ideation stage that determines how ideas are filtered, along with a rationale for how they are selected or rejected

When we say we value curiosity, this means we value thinkers who can imagine how the world of the future might be different than it is today, and we also value those who can ask exploratory questions that open up discussion. If your business is new to working with trends, these types of discussions might be unusual and even uncomfortable for some.

While trend leaders often readily embrace change, they do need to bring along stakeholders who might not be as comfortable with imagining life beyond the horizon. Trend leaders will almost always embrace change if they can see the impact it could make. From time to time, they will even push the boundaries and have an appetite for more radical change that drives real innovation.[28] You need to ensure you take your stakeholders – who may not naturally lean towards imaginative thinking – with you on the journey. This requires strong communication and leadership skills and the ability to paint a clear picture of the potential benefits of pursuing a trend and inspire confidence in the proposed direction.

Teams look to trend leaders to encourage them to embrace change, inspire them with a vision of the future, and lead the way in exploring new possibilities.

MEET THE TREND LEADER

Amelie Labarthe, Play Design Consultant, who was formerly Design Manager at The LEGO Group, describes how she benefitted from the energising influence of forward-thinking creative industry leaders that made an impact on her:

'I respect leaders who lead with vision and can share this spark of what the unknown could look like. Leaders who understand the importance of creating an emotional connection to the product. They make the future look like an adventure you want to hop on without a second thought. Great leaders to me

---

28   Duo Global Consulting, *Trend Leader Behavioural Study 2024*, commissioned by Joanna Feeley for the purpose of this book

understand what it takes to create a good creative team spirit, for innovation to thrive. They have always encouraged me to follow my instincts, it helped me have the confidence to dare to be the challenger.'[29]

You can play a vital role in fostering this culture by:

- Creating regular events and sessions to encourage collective exploration

- Valuing imaginative thinkers who can envision alternative futures, experiment and analyse risks

- Encouraging 'How might we...?' questions that spark open discussions

- Recognising that these types of discussions might be unfamiliar and potentially uncomfortable for some, requiring sensitivity and encouragement

Encourage divergent thinking

There are two different kinds of cognitive process, each serving different purposes when we're working with trends: divergent and convergent thinking. Divergent thinking is an exploratory process that involves generating multiple possibilities, ideation fluency and discovering unconventional solutions. It's useful for having ideas about what the future may hold. Some

29 Interview with Amelie Labarthe conducted on 29 October 2022 for the purpose of this book

people possess better divergent thinking abilities than others due to their natural cognitive make-up, but this skill can be developed through training and practice. Convergent thinking, on the other hand, is analytical, logical and focused on finding a single solution to a problem. It's useful for asking questions about trends and helping us knock ideas into shape and transform them from concepts into reality.

Each of these has a role to play in exploring future trends and their impacts on your business and customers. When we are forecasting future trends, we want to work with divergent thinkers first to benefit from their ability to think more broadly, then to work with convergent thinkers to identify blind spots, drill down into the details and discover issues.

When we're ideating and exploring trends, we need to prioritise divergent thinking in order that we consider a broad range of possibilities without being bogged down by how we'll execute them. Divergent thinking allows us to be open, and, critically, to imagine.

While we can gather data and research, this will only get us so far. If only it were as simple as assuming the future would be a logical extension of the past! None of us actually have the ability to *predict* the future, and it would be naïve to just extrapolate past events and assume the same patterns continue. We need to be able to imagine and create future opportunities, rather than predict a singular future. This is expressed perfectly by trend leader Talita Di Iorio, a senior consultant formerly of Google, Meta and X:

'I believe it's essential to educate stakeholders on the role of trends and futures. Trends get a bad reputation because people think this means we're talking about fads, as opposed to an opportunity to be leveraged, or a signal of a bigger movement, a piece of the zeitgeist. Futures, on the other hand, is a loaded term that makes people think of the work as "prediction", when it is not. We're not here to predict, but map out the possibilities.'[30]

Trend leaders see things with an 'unlimited possibilities mindset' and operate better when they are able to work at a more visionary level. There is a strong link between trend leadership and divergent thinking; 96% of trend leaders demonstrate a skew towards 'innovation and big-picture vision', reinforcing the point that trend leaders are predisposed to see (or imagine) possible future scenarios that others can't yet see.[31]

Additionally, 65% of trend leaders prefer 'choices' over 'procedure', which demonstrates they are more

---

30 Interview with Talita Di Iorio conducted on 28 February 2024 for the purpose of this book
31 Duo Global Consulting, *Trend Leader Behavioural Study 2024* (Duo Global Consulting, 2024), commissioned by Joanna Feeley for the purpose of this book

comfortable with free-flowing, exploratory, imaginative thinking and generating multiple solutions.[32]

When you're planning a trend kick-off or a group ideation session, think carefully about who you will need in the room to creatively explore the trends and imagine how they might apply to your business, categories and products. Design teams are usually well placed to think divergently, particularly if they have had formal design education or training where this skill will have been honed. You can pose open-ended questions to divergent thinkers, and it will prompt a wealth of new ideas.

Those contributing to trend discussions must be able to evaluate a trend from the *future* customer's perspective. Convergent thinkers, in contrast, will find it difficult to move beyond seeing how the customer acts or behaves *today*.

It is important to identify divergent thinkers and to collaborate with them, but you don't want to create a discussion environment in which there's no diversity of thought. Yes, convergent thinkers, with their preference for logic, may find it difficult to engage in brainstorming and answering, 'what if?' and 'how might we?' questions, but you can benefit from their objective analysis and desire for accuracy. Your trend-forecasting process will be all the more robust for it.

---

32 Ibid.

I have run many successful ideation workshops with a mix of divergent and convergent thinkers. I always start by sending a pre-meeting invite, directing attendees to an online tool to help them learn more about divergent and convergent thinking skills and understand where their natural preference sits. There are many of these freely available online. This is a good place to start when you're introducing your colleagues to using trends and explaining what type of thinking you value at different stages and why. It helps them feel included, and to know where their value in the process will lie.

You can mix groups of divergent (typically designers, insight, marketing or creative team members) and convergent thinkers (these are often buyers, merchandisers and technicians) to encourage a balance of perspectives. Use a discussion guide to explain the type of thinking you're looking for in a brainstorming session. Encourage new hypotheses; ideas should really push the boundaries, and you should be clear that you welcome even the most unconventional ideas. Keep in mind that, if you're looking to generate truly transformative and original ideas, you'll need to create an environment in which it is ok to share weird, disruptive and challenging ideas. According to Dator's Law, named after futurist Jim Dator of the University of Hawaii, 'Any useful idea about the future should appear to be ridiculous'. You don't need to worry about whether an idea is practical at this point, you can refine and add commercial guardrails later in the process.

Get your stakeholders working together in small groups and give them some future trend material to discuss and unpack, such as a trend report on a specific topic. At TrendBible, one of the most effective ways we encourage discussion when working with brands is to pose 'thought-starter' questions to drive curiosity based on the insights we've presented. For example, we might present a keynote on the future of inclusivity and diversity, and then host a workshop and pose a thought-starter question such as, 'How might you promote year-round inclusivity for the LGBTQ+ community beyond celebrating Pride month?'

MEET THE TREND LEADER

Even in a team full of problem-solving convergent thinkers, trend leader Ruby Sommer, Creative Manager at Northumbrian Water Group, found creative ways to fire up their divergent thinking.

When I interviewed her in 2024, Ruby shared a great example of how she ignited a sensory experience around her trend concepts, bringing them to life in such a way that her team could experience future ideas in a more tangible way:

'I created an immersive experience for my colleagues and allowed them to fully envisage what a trend could look, feel, smell and taste like. I hosted an ideation session and, before the event, I sent each delegate a preview pack with food samples, decorations and mini mood boards that reflected each of the trends I was going to explore. This took concept pitching to a new level for my company and is still talked about years later. It's even more impactful now two years on from the pitch, when they can see the trends coming to life in the real world.

'The experience helped me to better understand where I can channel my energy to really get the best colleague engagement and buy-in.'[33]

Creating inspiring events and touchpoints that generate excitement, anticipation and curiosity are a great foundation for prompting the right kind of explorative thinking among your stakeholders, ensuring you leave no stone unturned looking for your next big opportunity.

Welcome friction and counterargument

Correctly positioning a trend or new idea shouldn't be rushed, and it's important to make time to expose it to the scrutiny of others so you can see it from different perspectives to be sure you aren't operating in an echo chamber. Being willing to really probe a trend and see it from different angles and through different lenses helps us check its viability early on.

---

33 Interview with Ruby Sommer conducted on 31 January 2024 for the purpose of this book

If we fail to put a trend through its paces in the early stages, there's potential for problems to be discovered later on. Trends, by their nature, evolve and shape-shift, and we need to create processes that allow us to imagine what these changes might look like. It's impossible to imagine every eventuality, but it's much better to actively embrace the opportunity to stress-test a trend than not to bother. Otherwise, we may be at risk of bringing our own assumptions to a trend based on historical events, or our own inherent biases. Creating a space for a robust discussion is a useful means of helping a trend leader see things they can't yet see themselves.

Part of having a healthy conversation around a trend is creating space to generate and encourage counter-arguments. Conflict isn't something to avoid when we're dealing with trends, but some of your colleagues might find it strange or intimidating to raise contrary points or to disagree.

Clear guidelines detailing how people may bring counterarguments and engage in debate is critical to creating events that your colleagues look forward to. While you're not necessarily aiming for consensus, you will want to avoid people's ideas being shot down, and to record a fair debate that includes the pros and cons, upsides and downsides, and see what accelerating and decelerating factors might impact your proposed trend or idea.

Techniques for inviting conflict

One discussion technique for interrogating a new trend is to take a published trend report and ask a colleague to fulfil the role of 'Devil's Advocate', raising questions that intentionally challenge the prevailing view or mood around a trend. This provides a healthy scepticism and helps to see an emerging idea from a different angle. This will help you better anticipate how a trend might land with your audience in the real world and enables you to better plan how you'll respond to varying customer reactions.

Another technique is to host a pre-mortem ideation session. A pre-mortem gives you the space to identify issues and problems before they are a reality. It involves imagining a number of reasons why a trend might not land well with your customer, or perhaps why it may fail to come to fruition at all, and then working back from that to map out key sticking points in the journey which you can then set about removing.

Trend leaders are able to host these conversations and create spaces for everyone to share their thoughts and ideas respectfully. Though ultimately it may fall to you as trend leader to make the final decision and balance the commercial and creative aspects of a trend, this is a chance to gather more perspectives, and round-out your argument among a group of people who will likely know a lot about your company and customer base.

When you host these conversations, know that there will be a mixture of views in the room – some conservative and risk averse, others adventurous and open to change, but your job is to be swayed by neither. You will need to chair the conversation neutrally, encouraging debate and using questions as prompts to get the team to interrogate the trend being discussed.

Be mindful who you invite along to these discussions. I have seen companies ask employees to self-nominate to come along to trend discussions, which only ends up attracting the people who are already invested in trends. You need a cross-section of people and departments that enables you to listen to opinions from outside the echo chamber.

Identifying the right problem

Several years ago, I was asked to advise a paint company. Their product and marketing team briefed me with a seemingly simple task: to help them expand the colour range of their garden and outdoor paint products. The existing colour range consisted of a collection of brown shades and a forest green colour – pretty standard for an exterior paint range.

It was only once I started to ask questions about how the paint range fitted into their broader commercial strategic objectives that it became clear that we were trying to fix the wrong problem. Their strategic objectives were to differentiate themselves in an over-crowded market and to increase market share.

It was clear that adding another brown or green colour to their exterior paint collection wasn't going to improve their differentiation. I proposed a broader scope of work, looking at the garden and outdoor market more holistically. As a result, we found that 94% of choices made about home décor and DIY were being made by women (even if they weren't always the ones carrying out the work). Therefore, it was critical for the paint brand to connect on some level with their female consumers. How was I going to persuade this conservative brand, operating in a conservative (and masculine) market, to make a bold move and think in a transformational way, connecting with an audience they'd never connected with before?

I knew immediately that, as much as I might be able to inform and influence this bright, capable product and marketing team, I would need to equip them well enough to persuade their DIY stockists and retail partners to go on a new journey with them. They would need a rationale, a mutually beneficial business case, and the right language to be able to frame up (and attract) this new audience.

After profiling this new future consumer, we show-cased the proposed product direction, which included a recommendation to pick up on an early colour trend that was emerging at the time – grey.

Early nervous feedback included comments like, 'A grey paint looks like the undercoat you'd apply before you put the real colour on!' However, the marketing team's belief in the product began to grow. They went from saying, 'We can't do that!' to saying, 'How might we do that?' They exhibited curiosity. They grew more and more confident in their pitches to retailers. Months later, instead of having to constantly pitch new ideas to their retail partners, the retail partners began calling *them*, requesting new trend intelligence and asking whether there was anything else this team knew that could unlock opportunities in this undisrupted market. Needless to say, grey paint became their best-selling product and remained a top seller for over five years, chiming perfectly with a broader adoption of the trend across home, automotive, fashion and consumer products.

As a trend leader, you will often need to interrogate the brief you are given from key stakeholders in your business to ensure you're getting to the root of their issues and objectives.

There are often multiple problems a business is trying to solve, and paying attention to the right trends is only part of that conversation. Companies can often be working on strategic initiatives like increasing market share or refreshing their vision, and a trend leader with good access to – and awareness of – these initiatives can marry them together with any future market shifts that may help or hinder strategic decision making.

The relationship between company strategy and trends is always better when it's an open two-way channel. Firstly, trend leaders can weave the company's strategic priorities into the future trends where they are a good fit. For example, if a company is exploring a new corporate vision that includes being a market leader in sustainability, then the trend leader will include and discount trends in alignment with that goal. Secondly, the executive team can benefit from the trend intelligence and use it to inform company strategy. There should never be a gap between company strategy and future trends – they should be symbiotic and inform each other.

MEET THE TREND LEADER

In 2024, I asked Alex Post Miller, an experienced trend leader and currently Senior Researcher at Netflix, how she has identified the right problems when scoping out the areas of a business that require a focus on the future:

'This often comes from leadership to reinvigorate a struggling area of the business, or a strategic opportunity for growth or to bring in a new revenue stream. Sometimes, this can come from a business objective, or it can be inspired from a trend. That's one of the most exciting things about the trends space. You never know where a trend can take you. They can surprise you and motivate you to improve or pivot into a direction you were hoping for – or one you never anticipated.'[34]

---

34 Interview with Alex Post Miller conducted on 9 February 2024 for the purpose of this book

In an ideal scenario, there would be someone with a focus on the future at board level in every large company to ensure the focus is on the right problems, but the second-best scenario is an executive team that respects the value that an internal trend leader can bring and actively creates opportunities to collaborate with them.

Trend leaders help progressive companies to envision bold change and then make incremental steps to execute it.

Reflection and action points

1. Think of yourself as the host of conversations about trends – how might you invite the right people in at the right time to encourage involvement and engagement?

2. Be clear about when people can get involved in the trend process.

3. A healthy culture of curiosity means being open to new ideas.

4. When we're talking about trends, we're not just talking about material and shape; we can touch on some really big and important societal topics.

5. Use sourced trend material as a basis for driving deeper conversations.

6. Ask your executive team to share the company's strategic goals with you and help them understand how this will inform the trend selection process.

7. It's important to host healthy debates and handle challenges without clashing. Don't be afraid to issue both thinking and discussion guides to enable your teams to show up to workshops with the right mindset. Download our sample discussion guide from www.joannafeeley.com or simply scan the QR code at the end of this book to help you keep brainstorming sessions respectful and on-topic.

FIVE

Principle Three: Gather Trend Intelligence

H aving access to a variety of trend intelligence in the form of forecasts and reports is critical to spotting trends for your business and future audience. In most medium-to-large organisations, trend intelligence material is bought in from external providers. This can be in the form of trend presentations, trend subscriptions or working with consultants. Effective trend leaders get trend information to come to them, then they analyse and appropriate the information to fit their company's dynamics. You will need a variety of credible source points to help you spot the trends your business needs to act upon.

In this chapter, I will share how to gather information from credible sources to ensure you are properly informed, help you develop strategies for eliminating your blind spots, and how to mine trend intelligence from other progressive industries. You'll also need to know what to disregard – we'll talk about the value of deselecting trends in this chapter, too.

Gathering credible sources

It is because of their busy, multilayered role that trend leaders will benefit from being able to lean on trusted sources when it comes to anticipating change. The best trend leaders take a portfolio approach, commissioning trend forecasts from two or more trusted external agencies, working with consultants, purchasing published reports or trend subscriptions, and doing their own research.

Yes, I'm about to make a case for why it's so important to use an external trend agency, which I realise will come across as biased – but I say this from the perspective of someone who worked for many years inside companies as a trend leader myself. I know the value external trend insight brought to me, and I remember how busy the role of trend leader is.

Noise versus signals

What I learned from personal experience is that, in a large company, trend leaders simply can't devote sufficient time to create good-quality, immaculately evidenced, accurate forecasts. If they did, they would never get to the other critical aspects of their role.

While it's unrealistic to assume a trend leader will be able to set aside the time to consistently gathering and analysing signals of change themselves, an external trend partner or agency is scanning for them all the time. A dedicated trend agency might pick up twenty signals a day, which is over 7,000 signals per year, and are able to differentiate what is 'news' and what is a distinct indicator of forthcoming change.

Using an external trend partner isn't just due to time constraints, either. Distinguishing important signals from the background noise requires being permanently switched on to trends. To give an example, if you dip in and out of gathering trend intelligence, you can pick up on something that's new to you, but that in reality has been doing the rounds while you were focused on other things. Even if you are fortunate enough to have an internal foresight team in your company, building your external trend intelligence sources to spot new trends and track the pace of existing ones is critical if you are to validate and reinforce your decisions and eliminate your blind spots.

In today's noisy world of fake news and over-proliferation of content, the problem isn't that there is a shortage of information, it's that there's too much, and getting to the important bits is difficult.

How will you choose what to pay attention to, and how will you assess what's credible?

Credible sources

When you're gathering secondary trend intelligence, it needs to be reliable and accurate. Make sure:

- The source comes from a credible organisation, author or publication with expertise in the field

- There is transparency around how and where the research or information was collected and themed

- You cross-check any statistical data for accuracy and verify that it's recent

- The methodology underpinning the intelligence you have gathered is shared

When I talk about 'credible' information and trend sources, this isn't always something formal like a study published in an academic journal – some of the things that impact consumer confidence aren't true or real, but they impact how a consumer is feeling, nonetheless. It's entirely possible a customer can read something in the news that refers to a rise in the cost of living, and despite experiencing no real personal impact on their disposable income, will still make plans to pull back on their spending. Watch out for the link – or the gap – between what's driving change and what people are actually doing.

For a clear picture of the future and to be properly informed, companies need:

- Big-picture social and systems change reporting – collecting intelligence from the likes of Dubai Futures Forum, the World Economic Forum, Anticipation Conference, United Nations Climate Change Conference, to name just a few – all of which would be supplied, synthesised and appropriated to your company by a good external trend partner

- Cultural and consumer lifestyle reporting (including synthesised Macro Trend reports that tell you how your audience will be living, outlining what's shaping their needs, hopes, ambitions, desires and aspirations)

- Product-specific trend direction (covering material, colour, finish and product trends)

- Global trade show reporting

- Global and regional market reviews

- Competitor analysis

- Bespoke deep dives into specific business challenges, for example if your company's goal is to get to carbon zero, you might commission intelligence informing carbon zero initiatives

Cite your sources

A strong trend leader isn't tempted to feel like they must personally have all the answers, but they recognise the importance of being properly informed by having access to credible forecasting resources and external perspectives. You will always be asked to give assurances and certainty and to 'predict', and a good part of the role of trend leader is balancing what (little) information you have with the confidence to act on incomplete information and handle ambiguity.

Citing multiple credible sources in your trend presentations, or when asked, can make the difference between your colleagues believing in the trend or not. Someone who is worried about a new direction or is looking at a new trend for the first time will need extra reassurance that this trend is going to happen, that it is going to resonate with your customer, and that it is going to be commercially relevant for the business. You will find that different departments in your business need different levels of reassurance when applying trend findings.

Early on in my career, I was delivering a future trend presentation to a senior management team when one of the board members asked where I'd got a statistic from. He said he didn't rate the global market research company I had quoted and tried to use that as grounds for dismissing a whole trend. Although this certainly put me off my stride, I was able to cite other credible source points to reinforce their belief in the trend. If your process is airtight, you'll have several reasons why the trend you're presenting is valid. Having a strong justification for why a trend will be important means being able to back it up using multiple sources, data sets and reasons, known as 'triangulating' your research. Triangulation stabilises the trend and grounds it, meaning that you have many reasons to believe it will become a reality, and in the event of one of your strands of research not coming to fruition, the trend doesn't fall down altogether.

Getting a broader view

There may be times in your career when you may have to explain to senior budget holders why you need external resources to support your internal capabilities. I have known companies cut their external trend spend because they feel like their internal design team ought to be doing this as part of their job, and this leads to the gradual creation of a blinkered, company-centric view of the world where you risk missing something new and important.

As an external trend partner, it's my job to make sure my clients have access to trend intelligence, so that they can plug it into their plans and connect it to their customer. Being aware of upcoming changes is a business-critical activity. Someone inside your business needs to be doing this, and it's never a bad idea to ask who is responsible for it. We're a little while away from having a Chief Futures Officer in every large corporate business, and until we do, you need to make sure you're crystal clear on how your company scopes out and invests in future opportunities.

Segmenting, categorising and clustering intelligence

Once you've got a flow of credible trend information coming to you, it's a good idea to use a system to make sense of it. This isn't a comprehensive guide on how to forecast your own trends; however, I will share a few frameworks that my clients have found useful to help them stay on track and know what to pay attention to.

Gathering multiple trend resources is an important first step, but there is undoubtedly work to do in synthesising this into a comprehensive future picture for your business. This involves:

- Finding the commonalities among the published forecasts

- Identifying outlier ideas that you think might be interesting for your customers

- Understanding when on the timeline this trend will have peak relevance for your customers

- Spotting any opportunities for refreshing existing elements of your strategy or product range

A good trend leader organises their trend material and provides guidance and signposting for their colleagues.

Trends are multifaceted and are an accumulation of signals from a number of places. They can come from obvious societal changes, like a rise in people choosing to live in cities, to almost imperceptible shifts in people's decision-making processes.

I like to use three frameworks that work like 'buckets', which you can fill with different types of information to help you determine:

1. What is driving change

2. Who is changing

3. When change is coming

Let's take a look at each of these in turn.

1. PESTELE – what is driving change?

Consumers' attitudes and behaviours are influenced by change that is happening on a broad scale, so when we're forecasting future trends, it's important to be able to zoom out and see the bigger picture. Change

comes from several elements, including politics, eco-
nomics, society, technology, the environment, the law
and ethics (referred to as PESTELE, or STEEPLE).
Changes in these domains can be small or large, obvious or hidden, interconnected or dispersed, compli-
mentary or frictional. These act as catalysts for new
consumer attitudes and expectations.

You can gather examples of changes in each category
of PESTELE and then find commonalities among
them, and then cluster them by theme. For example,
an emerging theme might be 'privacy', and you could
demonstrate a growing adoption of this trend by evidencing a rise in activism relating to protecting privacy, shifts in how people use and trust technology,
and forthcoming privacy legislation etc.

2. Pyramid of Influence – who is changing?

Trends gather pace and accumulate an audience over
time. They are adopted among smaller, more adventurous consumers first, and then spread to bigger
and more traditional and mainstream groups. The
Pyramid of Influence is a model I use, which maps
different types of consumers and their appetite for
change across five groups: Mavens, Early Adopters,
Early Majority, Late Majority and Laggards.[35]

35 Based on the trend adoption curve popularised by Everett Rogers,
in his book *The Diffusion of Innovation* (Free Press, 1962), building on
the work of French sociologist Gabriel Tarde in the late nineteenth
century

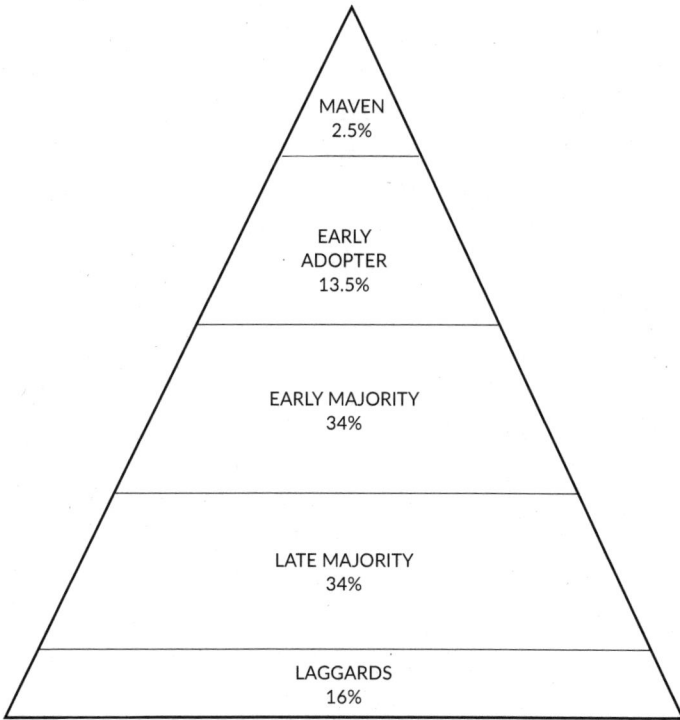

The Pyramid of Influence

According to the model, Mavens make up 2.5% of society, and are the most progressive group, instigating change and solving problems themselves.[36] Early Adopters make up 13.5% and are those who seek out new and better ways to do things and are happy to experiment. The Early Majority make up 34%, are more risk averse and need more convincing about

---

36 The word 'maven' comes from the Yiddish word meyvn, which means 'one who understands'

trying or buying something new, but they are critical in tipping a trend into mass appeal. The Late Majority audience also make up 34% of the market and are much more traditional, requiring more persuasion to do something new. They need to see trends being lived or adopted directly within their close trusted network and repeatedly referenced in multiple trusted media sources. Lastly, Laggards make up 16% of consumers and are usually only prepared to change habits and behaviours out of necessity because their preferred ways become obsolete.

Each of these groups has different psychological factors. Their needs, intentions, beliefs and motivations are different. For example, a Maven audience is typically trying to find a solution to an unmet need or problem, while an Early Adopter might be seeking out 'coolness' or currentness, and a Late Majority audience can be seeking out sameness from a need to 'fit in'.

These different categories are often misinterpreted as fixed personality traits rather than context-dependent behaviours that vary across different innovations. It is important to consider your own industry, categories and brand, and then overlay each adoption group to map out which groups correspond most strongly. This won't give you a scientific way to group your customers, but it is a system for spotting when change is impacting a group further up (or down) the chain, and to anticipate when it will influence your core customer base. Remember, it's entirely possible that an

Early Adopter will have moved on to something new by the time an idea lands with the Late Majority. It's often the case with style-driven products that Early Adopters will see mass-market adoption of a trend as a reason in itself to move on to something different and more unusual.

It's worth noting that there is no hard and fast rule about how quickly a trend or new idea moves through these groups – it can be days, months or years, but the only way to track the pace is to have a constant eye on what – and who – is changing.

3. Weak Signals – when is change coming?

Having captured the big-picture shifts that are driving change in your PESTELE framework, it's a good idea to also capture 'weak signals', which are a different type of indication that something new is coming.

Trend forecasting relies on spotting these 'weak signals' of change – the early pieces of information that demonstrate something new is happening. They can be novel, surprising, challenging and contradict the status quo. They can be a smattering of data points, statistics or individual innovations – and clustering these into themes builds a picture of new and emerging patterns, attitudes or behaviours. For example, let's imagine you have a company that makes artificial plants and flowers, and you spot weak signal – a new indoor irrigation system that has been listed as an innovation on a start-up platform like Crowdfunder or Indigogo that you think signals a new type of approach to indoor gardening. You also spot a study that suggests that having a certain type of plant in your home has been scientifically proven to lower stress. These weak signals can be grouped to identify emerging risks and opportunities; can you spot if the business is facing any new or underplayed risk? How might your business turn this into an opportunity?

Individual weak signals can be interesting in themselves, but you will need a group of them to provide sufficient evidence to your business that this is a broader movement and not just a one-off invention. You can build an evidence file for these to monitor how the trend grows and morphs from weak signal (three to four inventions) to strong market evidence (adopted by niche brands and of interest to Early Adopters).

WATCH OUT

It's important for trend leaders to be able to remember that interesting future ideas aren't always the ones getting the most airtime. News and social media have their own agendas and can accelerate and blow up a weak signal so that, at a surface level, it may seem to be more significant than it actually is. Ground your trends properly with evidence of big-picture lifestyle drivers, connect them to the right early audiences and link these to weak signals to create as robust a foundation as possible.

Competitor analysis

It is often the case that a company that hasn't yet invested in any trend forecasting will be relying solely on competitor analysis (or 'comp shopping' as it's known in the retail sector) as their only source of market or trend intelligence. Evaluating what your competitors are making, selling and saying is always worthwhile to give you a snapshot of 'now', but it will not help you understand the future trading context or upcoming shifts in consumer behaviour.

There is a big difference between strategic competitor analysis (comparing what your competitors have developed and why, and evaluating whether this has resonated with the intended audience), and the act of looking for new product development ideas that will resonate with your *future* consumer. Companies often muddle the two and look to competitors to inform their own new product development ideas, which is a misleading and flawed practice in many ways.

The products that we see on the shelf today were researched and designed two or more years ago, for a social context and commercial rationale that was anticipated and planned for – two or more years ago. Progressive companies work ahead to plan products and messaging that are immaculately timed to coincide with the customer behaviours that they had projected. Forecasting too close to 'now conditions' isn't an advisable approach, but copying your competitor's products doesn't classify as trend forecasting at all.

When competitor analysis is being used as a start point for innovation by your company, you are at risk of copying what will ultimately end up being an outdated strategy. More importantly, this still isn't helping you with the job of understanding what it is that *your* customer will want in two years' time.

So, what is a good use of competitor analysis when it comes to trends? Ask yourself these questions:

- What did your competitors develop and why?

- Has the strategy, product selection or messaging done its job?

- What was the objective? To resonate with an existing audience, to attract a new audience, to shift consumers towards a new way of consuming or shopping, to test out a new material or production process?

- How have your competitors succeeded by anticipating future needs and how does this compare with what your company produced in the same window of opportunity?

- What do you think their innovation strategy is, and how does yours compare?

Performing competitor analysis or conducting a 'comp shop' can also be an effective way to make a business case for working further ahead. You can demonstrate which competitors adopted which trends and use this intelligence not simply to answer the question 'What did they do?', but more importantly, 'What did we miss and why?'

Identifying your blind spots and biases

Blind spots and biases can create an area of weakness for even the most seasoned trend professionals. These cognitive limitations can lead companies to miss crucial trends, exclude potential audiences and make costly misjudgements. However, by implementing robust processes to identify and mitigate these issues, businesses can significantly enhance their trend intelligence and decision-making capabilities.

Blind spots are areas of oversight or ignorance that prevent us from seeing the full picture, while biases are preconceived notions that can skew our judgement. In trend forecasting, these can manifest as gaps in trend intelligence or unconscious prejudices that influence decision making.

No individual is immune to having blind spots and we all carry unconscious bias, it's a natural part of how our brains work. We make split-second judgements based on our own personal experiences, cultural influences and what we may see as 'societal norms' – and these may not be objectively fair or true. However, when we are making decisions on behalf of a large company, we are responsible for impacting millions of different customers and our work must be as inclusive as possible.

The risks are amplified if:

- You haven't got a process for spotting the change that's happening in other industries, regions, countries or cultures

- You're working with a narrow customer profile or persona instead of thinking about mindsets and characteristics that allows for a deeper understanding of the diversity that exists in your customer base

- You aren't regularly and systematically evaluating your assumptions about your customers and looking for changes in your target customers' lives

The importance of diversity in trend forecasting

By embracing diverse perspectives, you can ensure your forecasts are not just accurate, but truly representative of the complex, multicultural world in which we live.

Customer personas are a shorthand widely used by companies to define their target audience. However, to ensure they are representative and inclusive, these profiles must be thoroughly examined for socioeconomic, disability, race, religion, age, sexual orientation and gender inclusion (this is not an exhaustive list).

If a trend starts life without being examined for its breadth of application across different types of consumers, we risk designing products and messaging that exclude and offend. When inclusivity is at the heart of the design process, it really shows.

An excellent example of this is household product brand OXO, which is widely recognised for its inclusive design philosophy. They use universal design principles that make everyday products accessible and usable for everyone, ensuring that items are easy to grip, hold and manipulate for people with disabilities, older adults and those with limited dexterity, such as people with arthritis or muscle weakness. They also invest in research and development to ensure that they are staying abreast of latest assistive design technologies and methodologies.

In the words of Disability Research Fellow Dr Jo Gooding:

'All elements of the design process have an important role to play, and it is imperative to build in a willingness to engage with different perspectives. The simplest advice is to design "with, not for". This is applicable to all social groups, but within disability there is a mantra "nothing about us, without us". Innovation teams should use human-centred co-design, not simulations, and actively invite the perspectives of people with lived experiences at the start, and throughout, the process.'[37]

How might we eliminate blind spots and biases?

One strategy to mitigate your blind spots and biases is to seek out perspectives that challenge your assumptions by inviting people with different lived experiences, diverse voices, different views into your innovation and trend process. Purposefully look for contrarian views to help you see a trend or idea from multiple alternative angles and challenge your assumptions.

Make sure you ask your external trend partners about their inclusivity and diversity practices, and how they gather their research and develop their hypotheses. For example, at TrendBible, we have a Framework for Fairness, which we have crafted to share with our clients so that they can see how and where we source our imagery and what our inclusivity and diversity guidelines are. We speak with experts and people with specific lived experiences so that we don't end up forecasting a trend about adaptive home environments, for example, without asking a wheelchair

---

37 Interview with Dr Jo Gooding conducted on 2 February 2024 for the purpose of this book

user, or developing a design trend steeped in Latin American culture without having someone with Latin American heritage vet the trend for insensitivities or cultural appropriation.

Acknowledging and actively working to overcome blind spots and biases is not just about improving trend forecasting – it's about creating a more inclusive, innovative and successful business environment.

Cross-pollinating innovation

In trend terms, cross-pollination is when a trend transfers from one audience, sector or geography to another. It can be as simple as a consumer accessing a new and convenient improvement to one aspect of their lives – say, paying for their groceries with iris-scanning technology, and then expecting this new level of service the next time they want to unlock their front door or access their medical records.

The most important thing is that you're not blinkered into only seeing in-category innovation and can recognise that shifts in consumer behaviour elsewhere are worth paying attention to.

In 2018, if you were manufacturing laundry detergent, sofas or nail polish, and you'd only been monitoring trends inside your own sector, it may have come as a surprise to you when veganism started to transition out of the food industry and into non-food products, as shoppers began to demand transparency about what ingredients were in everything they were using – from moisturiser to weed killer.

Veganism cross-pollinated from being a food trend into many other sectors, and even those who were not vegetarians or vegans in terms of the food they ate, started to become aware of what animal products were used inside their favourite beauty and home cleaning brands. Suddenly, the knowledge that an animal fat was used as a surfactant in your favourite shampoo didn't seem so appealing. Armed with new information, consumers started to rethink their product choices, which had huge consequences for some of the world's biggest manufacturers, who had to recalibrate the chemistry of their products at short notice.

New laundry brands such as Smol were able to gain valuable market share simply by educating consumers, dialling up their vegan and cruelty free messaging and calling out traditional laundry agents which used rendered fat from animals.

Consumers do not think in silos; they will migrate a newly acquired set of values or behaviours across other parts of their lives. So, naturally, trend leaders must also avoid thinking in silos.

Companies are typically good at monitoring the outputs of their direct competitors, understanding who else competes in their market and what their unique selling point (USP) is. However, your customers' views of your product aren't solely shaped by how it stacks up against the next thing on the shelf. They learn newer, better, faster and more efficient ways to do things from the products and experiences they consume elsewhere, and wonder why they can't get that same product functionality or experience from you.

Breakthrough innovations often come from outside your industry. Just as consumers look outside of a category for new ways of doing things, so do innovative brands.

Founder of letterbox flower delivery company Bloom & Wild, Aron Gelbard, disrupted the flower delivery industry by taking inspiration from the snack industry:

> 'I was an addict of Graze, the snack subscription company, and started to wonder whether we could do flowers through the letterbox, and if that would make the delivery experience better. They used the letterbox delivery as a really nice hook which made for a talking point in its own right.'[38]

Despite not pioneering the concept, they were able to use cross-pollination to popularise the idea,

---

38 The Challenger Project, *How Bloom & Wild Built a Challenger Brand in a Commodity Market* (eatbigfish, 2022), https://thechallengerproject. com/blog/2017/aron-gelbard-interview, accessed 9 April 2025

which led Bloom & Wild to become Europe's largest direct-to-consumer flower delivery company only a few short years after its inception.

How to use cross-pollination strategies

- Seek out new attitudes or behaviours in other trending sectors.

- Use cross-pollination as an innovation tool, to help you borrow behaviours from other sectors and see if they bring a fresh perspective or new place to innovate in your industry.

- Trends cross-pollinate from country to country, too. Make sure you consume trend intelligence from different countries to the one you're operating in as trends can build momentum elsewhere first.

- Encourage collaborative ideation and invite colleagues to share examples of innovations that could transfer to your industry.

- Use a brainstorming format and then cluster and rank the ideas in terms of a) the likelihood that they will impact your industry and b) those that could drive innovation for your business.

Trend leaders are responsible for identifying change both inside and outside of their industry, and implementing regular cross-industry analysis can create huge opportunities for driving innovation.

The art of deselection

There may be hundreds, if not thousands, of trends live at any given time. It's impossible, and ill-advised, to act upon all of them. It can be daunting, but you will need to actively discount a number of trends and demonstrate why they aren't right for your company.

Making good-quality decisions on when to deselect a trend, idea or concept is a critical skillset of the trend leader. You will ultimately have to make choices about which ideas you progress now, and which you park for later, or perhaps even choose to drop them forever. Deselecting a trend does not mean the trend itself lacks value. It may even be something your competitors can succeed with but which is off-brand for your audience, or that clashes with your specific timeframes, production limitations or geographical focus.

It's important to have as much knowledge as possible about everything that's going on in the world, but that doesn't mean you should act upon all of it. You must select the specific trends that have true alignment with your business and future customer – trends that you can execute with authenticity and that are congruent with what your company aspires to be known for.

Deselecting trends is valuable because it demonstrates a clear and intentional focus. It allows you to articulate the distinction between knowledge and action: understanding what's changing and deciding whether this warrants action for your business. You will need this because, from time to time, your colleagues will bring trends to your attention that you may need to evaluate, and you will need to share your rationale for not progressing with them.

Some trends will be easy to spot and back – perhaps they will have hallmark characteristics of a trend that brought success to your business in the past. Others will be a stretch for your customer and your business and will take them on a journey towards something that's new for them. Newness can sometimes be profiled as a risk inside a large corporate business, although the journey to the next multimillion-dollar innovation never starts out as a guaranteed bet.

Here are some guiding questions to help you evaluate whether you should pursue a trend:

- Does the trend align with your core business values and goals?

- Does it allow you to experiment with attracting a new potential customer base?

- Is it feasible using your current product development processes and tooling?

- Does it give you a competitive edge?

- Does it fulfil an unmet customer need?

- Does it give you a long-term opportunity, or is it a chance to capitalise on a short-term fad?

- Can you execute authentically and credibly?

WATCH OUT

When you deselect a trend, make sure you have scrupulously documented the whole process. It is vital to keep a record of the date the idea was parked, and the reason why. This way, you have a record of the agreement not to progress the idea, which you may need to reference should your competitors get traction with this trend. This still doesn't mean it was right for you, but a competitor generating a lot of attention will make people inside your business wonder if you made the right call.

Deselecting trends, just like selecting them, should be something to discuss. Make sure you have communicated with the appropriate team members all the way through the process. Your job as trend leader will usually be to make the call about whether you go ahead with a trend or not, and it's wise to keep a record of the conversations and judgements that informed that decision.

Reflection and action points

1. Make sure you have a range of trend intelligence coming into your business to help you stay informed and be able to distinguish noise from news, and trends from fads.

2. Make sure you look beyond your direct competitors and keep an eye on other industries

to stay ahead of the curve and meet evolving consumer demands.

3. Run a workshop looking at established attitudes and behaviours in other industries. What can your team spot that could cross-pollinate over to your sector? Is there an opportunity to lead on this for your company?

4. Trend leaders should welcome a broad awareness of all trends but should only select those that can be executed with authenticity and close alignment to their company's goals and values, and without cultural appropriation.

5. How might you design a 'nothing about us, without us' approach to inclusion?

6. It's essential to justify to colleagues why certain trends are not being pursued.

SIX

Principle Four: Contextualise Your Trends

When we contextualise a trend, we are thinking more deeply into the detail of how a trend will perform across different consumers and demographics, which geographies will be most and least receptive, and how big and impactful a trend is going to be.

In this chapter, we will look at how to give a trend the best chance of success by building the future context around the trend.

There are five methods by which you can stress-test and contextualise your trends, and we will look at each of them in turn:

1. Who: consumer mindset.

2. Where: regional nuances.

3. When: timing is everything.

4. When: take the temperature.

5. How: the Timeless/Timely Index.

The Catalysts of Change model and the consumer mindset

Trend leaders need to be able to anticipate a trend before it can be evidenced through audience behaviour or other tangible means like statistical data. They must persuade their colleagues to invest in it before any concrete signs of its existence can be found.

So how can you build confidence among your stakeholders without hard evidence of a behavioural change?

Psychology tells us that before someone's behaviour has shifted, they must first have changed the way they think. One of the best ways to map the journey of a future trend is to understand the mind of the consumer and examine the thoughts and emotional triggers that drive the desire for change in the first place.

To do this, you will need to peel back the layers even further and understand what informs and influences these thoughts and emotions.

The Catalysts of Change™ model, which I developed for my clients at TrendBible, is a useful and practical way to map the cascade of influencing factors and identify potential opportunities.

Here is how to use each segment of the model. You can access a template framework to map out your own Catalysts of Change by scanning the QR code at the back of this book.

1. Catalysts

Catalysts are a series or group of social, cultural and economic drivers that are synthesised together. They prompt changes in taste and shape new thought patterns. Catalysts are made up of a mix of Mega Trends and Macro Trends, which differ in scope and duration.

Mega Trends are long-term, global shifts or transformative forces that shape society over a period of around twenty-five years. Examples of Mega Trends are things like urbanisation, climate change or the ageing population.

Macro Trends are medium-term shifts influencing lifestyles and consumer mindsets over two-to-five-year periods. A Macro Trend is a clustering of influences that can include elements of Mega Trends mixed with calculable events; these are timely social, economic and cultural cues, such as upcoming movies, books, exhibitions, events and innovations.

Catalysts create a context and mood which drive consumer attitudes, that subsequently shape behaviours. Mapping this cascade of influence helps you better anticipate how a mindset shift might play out and alter your audience's future behaviours. Progressive companies constantly gather evidence of catalysts and have the confidence to act when they sense attitudinal shifts – not behavioural shifts.

This approach is not without challenges for organisations that rely heavily (or exclusively) on data, market research and copying competitors. Many companies are happy to gift the commercial advantage to their competitors, to let them innovate, while they themselves wait for trends to fully emerge in the market before they act. The consequence of this is that a progressive customer or competitor is ten steps ahead and has already moved on by the time a more passive or reactive company responds to what is now 'old news'.

A great way to form unique and dynamic catalysts is to clash Mega and Macro trends together in abstract and unusual ways. For example, you could blend two pieces of information – a projected increase in people living in urbanised areas (Mega Trend), mixed with a rise in communities pooling their resources like home improvement tools and surplus groceries (Macro Trend), and ideate around what attitudes and behaviours that this collision might spark. This is a useful way to help brands identify new 'white spaces' they might create for themselves to dominate the market.

If you don't have an internal trend or foresight team, consider partnering with an external trend partner to provide you with catalysts to enable you to work at pace and in sufficient depth.

2. Attitudes

What will your audience be thinking and feeling in the future?

Working with the future is, in part, social science – understanding human behaviour and how groups change their thoughts and beliefs and express new needs. To contextualise your trends, you will need to understand the consumer mindset that is triggering new emotions and new opinions, that will in turn spark new types of behaviour.

When you are thinking about your future consumer, think about identifying mindsets and characteristics rather than set personas or demographics. This is because it's too easy to stereotype if we focus on attributing a set of attitudes or behaviours to a particular age group, gender or ethnicity.

The main factors shaping the consumer mindset are:

- Psychological (motivation, intention, attitude, perception, conformity, compensatory behaviours, the mechanics of making and breaking new habits, the interplay between uncertainty and risk)

- Social (family, reference groups, persuaders and influencers, aspirations, status and roles)

- Personal factors (age, economic class or status, values system, cultural dimensions, the impact of biases)

These aspects generate thought patterns and stimulate emotions which ultimately guides consumers' purchasing choices, influences their decision making and steers their behaviours.

Even if your customer isn't an Early Adopter, you need to know when their attitudes have shifted and what caused that to happen. Capturing the zeitgeist and finding golden opportunities, means understanding the origins of consumer decision making, and anticipating how tastes will develop and change.

3. Behaviours

Seeing consumers live out a new behaviour is deeply comforting. It's hard evidence that a trend is being lived out. However, waiting for consumers to exhibit demonstrable signs of a behavioural change is extremely late in the trend-development process. When this happens, it means that the trend has already arrived. While some companies can still make some money and retain some relevance by riding the coattails of a trend that's already fully emerged, waiting for others to innovate first is not a safe place to be in the modern world.

As an example of a behaviour shift, let's unpick the rise in people partaking in cold-water swimming.

We can see their behaviour has demonstrably changed – going for a swim in a lake or investing in an at-home ice bath. This behaviour was shaped by new thoughts, and if we peel back the layers, we can investigate (with hindsight) what was influencing this shift in thoughts. What altered their attitudes and values to cause such a trend?

Catalysts for the change included things like a study detailing the health benefits of a cold-water therapy, a newspaper article about the positive effects of cold therapy on post-exercise recovery, and, latterly, a TV documentary about extreme athlete and self-proclaimed 'iceman' Wim Hoff. It is 'drip-drip' effects like these that mean that consumer values – and therefore behaviours – are shaped over time, often without us consciously recognising it.

Consequently, interest in cold-water therapy grew 600% as a search term between 2019 and 2024, and the sales of ice baths saw a 925% increase in sales in the UK over the same period. It is expected to be valued as a twelve-billion-dollar industry by 2030.

4. Opportunities

Mapping this cascade of influence from catalysts, to attitude, to behaviour, means you can anticipate change and identify opportunities early. You can use the Catalysts of Change model to identify whitespace, or untapped market potential.

A good first step is to go through the motions of mapping this trend cycle as if you were going to action it, and involving all of the appropriate stakeholders. That way, you can track the trend in real-time, seeing evidence of how the consumer mindsets shifted, evidencing related behaviours and even collecting examples of other brands' responses to the same trend, all of which will build confidence in the process. This will help you persuade your stakeholders to have the courage to create a response the moment you identify your catalyst or spot a shift in attitude.

5. Decision stacking

Consumers make decisions based on a wide range of influences, some of which have nothing to do with how your category is typically shopped. They respond to a blend of (sometimes conflicting) influences, and 'stack' their decisions by weighing up and ordering their values, and it's their non-negotiable values that become the ones they base their decision on.

One such example is luxury scented candles, a category that has enjoyed huge growth over several years but where there is nervousness about how healthy they are (given that home fragrance and candle fragrance have now been described as a pollutant equivalent to second-hand cigarette smoke). Stacked on top of this health risk is the rising cost of living, which starts to position expensive candles as non-essential purchases, and suddenly the customer has two compelling reasons to change their attitude towards them. Ensure you think about decisions your audience is making in both parallel and unrelated categories, and look for evidence of these being stacked on top of decisions they typically make about your product.

Regional nuances

The next method by which you can stress-test and contextualise your trend is by looking at regional nuances. Most global brands want to be able to create products and messaging that resonate with customers anywhere and everywhere. They seek to eliminate anything that will limit their ability to scale to a global level. This includes anything that skews a product range or idea to a particular market – I refer to this as a regional nuance. A regional nuance can be a custom, religion, historic stigma, symbol, cultural belief or even just a quirk that is specific to a location, culture or country.

When you are contextualising future trends, it's important you think ahead of time about how a trend will land with the various markets your company serves. If you deliver a product that doesn't resonate in a certain region, at best you'll be left with a ton of product that didn't sell, and at worst, you could end up with a huge amount of bad press and even a legal situation on your hands.

Whether it's a colour, motif, symbol, phrase or the whole design aesthetic, you need to be clear about which markets your trend will enter, and which regional nuances apply *before* you embark upon your design and product development phase. A regional nuance evaluation will help pre-determine how a trend will be perceived by the end customer. How detailed your exploration is can vary – some companies commission a cultural deep-dive in every country they cater to, others appoint customer focus groups to listen for regional nuances they might have missed, and some establish a set of rules per region to help guide employees in their decision making.

My team and I once worked with a Chinese luxury bedding brand that recognised that their domestic customers were increasingly investing in European brands and wanted to explore the possibility of including a more Euro-centric design aesthetic. We embarked on an extensive discovery phase, spending time in Shanghai, Chengdu and Beijing, visiting scores of people's homes to understand each region's décor, influence and aesthetic, working with a Chinese cultural anthropologist and getting an understanding of the retail scene. As part of this process, our client embarked on a European inspiration trip, where my team hosted a tour of all the best luxury to mid-range bedding brands and retailers in London and Paris. Our objective was to reach an agreement from both parties about what a 'European aesthetic' really meant.

Of course, we included a visit to one of the UK's most successful mid-range bedding companies, The White Company, whose white cotton bedding was extremely popular in the UK, where white bedding was a top seller and had become a symbol of minimalistic luxury. However, in the Chinese market, white sheeting – and indeed the colour white itself – is symbolic of death, sorrow and grief.

Had we omitted the regional nuances and in-depth research and advised this Chinese brand to include white bedding in their collection, we would have set them up for failure. Instead, we were able to have a sensible conversation about how to respond to the appetite for European design and channel this into the design process.

Experience has taught me that brands often care too little about the regional flavours, tastes, customs and quirks, and in their haste to create a singular brand offer that caters for everyone, they miss the opportunity to build a brand that really connects with customers.

Here are three strategies for accommodating regional nuances I have successfully implemented for global brands.

- **Strategy 1: Create a regional nuances guide.** Produce a guidance document that describes regional nuances in the markets you serve and help your design team quickly sense-check their concepts and designs against a set of guidelines to enable them to work at pace, and to promote autonomy among the design team. Make sure the guide is refreshed annually, because nuances can morph and shift and new ones can emerge. It's important that the guide becomes part of the training process for new staff, too.

- **Strategy 2: Create region-specific ranges or messaging.** Another successful strategy I've seen work well is developing product collections specific to key regions. This might not be easy to do for every country when you're a global brand, but if there are important nuances in a particular market, you may be able to make a business case for creating part of a range that speaks directly to that nuance. I've seen a South African homeware retailer do this successfully, collaborating with independent Indigenous South African designers to produce homeware collections to sit alongside their mainstream commercial offering to celebrate South African heritage and craft.

- **Strategy 3: Co-develop regional interpretations.**
  I once worked with a parent company that
  owned a suite of brands across the Nordic
  countries and had been issuing a single set of
  trends to cover the whole region. This left no
  room to add a country-specific flavour to make
  the trends fully resonate. What felt tasteful
  for the Swedish market felt boring to Finnish
  consumers. To appropriate the trends to each
  country, my team and I co-developed regional
  interpretations of the trends with representatives
  of the brand from six territories. The designers
  took the parts of the master suite of trends that
  they felt fit their region the best and we were able
  to work with them to ensure they were getting
  a good balance between being progressive
  enough and not staying too safe, all while staying
  sensitive to local specifics.

If you have multiple territories you need to cater to,
try hosting a workshop with representatives from
each in one room so that you can adhere to a central
product development strategy while also being sensitive to the needs of each region.

If it's in the hands of trend leaders to lead positive
change, then taking time to understand, respect and
amplify the culture and traditions in the regions that
global companies operate in is a huge opportunity to
do so.

Timing is everything

You need to be as sure as possible that the trends you select and use in your business are timed to coincide with your audience's readiness for them. Being first to market with a trend can be just as catastrophic as being too late. If you have an audience predominantly made up of those with an Early Adopter mindset, they will have an appetite for novelty and new ideas and will act fast to be among the first to embrace it. If you have a more traditional audience with a Late Majority mindset, they will better respond to a trend once they've had the chance to see it bed into the market, having taken comfort in seeing their friends and family adopt it first.

What we know to be true is that mass-market customers warm up to trends over time, and they need to see, hear and feel a trend unfold, soaking up multiple signals and building awareness as other groups around them adopt it.

As we explored in Chapter Five, if you have successfully anchored your trend and found some weak signals that point to its emergence across multiple industries, your customer will pick up on these too as the trend builds in the market. As it comes to life, signals emerge from all around you as the trend grounds itself in different areas, such as food, architecture, technology, film and literature. For a mass-market audience, the more anchored the trend, the more belief they will build and the more likely they will be to act upon it.

For example, a trend like 'the optimised self' (where consumers seek to measure their health to unlock peak performance) is anchored in the emergence of wearable health-tracking technology, the growth of the nootropics category, the number of online articles about functional food and beverages, the emergence of ingestible beauty products, and a flurry of 'food as medicine' TV shows and books being published. The consumer receives messages from multiple sources that this trend is important. Those with an Early Adopter mindset will be among the first to respond to this trend, and then, months – or even years – later, as the trend gets fully embedded into everyday life, the Early and Late Majority are persuaded to make changes to their lives.

So although you may well have an audience of Mavens or Early Adopters that will 'get' your trend early, it won't fully have meaning for a mass-market Late Majority customer until those social and cultural cues – events, films, books, TV shows – come to life and make their impression.

Anticipating the right time to strike for your audience's change in attitude or behaviour is a critical skill and the consequences of getting it wrong can be costly.

How does a trend leader time their trends well?

- Develop knowledge of your audience breakdown – what percentage of them have an Early Adopter mindset? How many of them have a Late Majority mindset? If you are unsure, take the Consumer Mindset quiz by scanning the QR code at the back of this book.

- Know where your customer gets influenced – who inspires them and encourages them to adopt a new attitude or behaviour, or to try something new? How long does your customer typically take to act once these influencers express the adoption of a new trend?

- What is your company's role in making customers feel safe to invest in a new way of doing things? How might you build and engender trust to help them try something new?

MEET THE TREND LEADER

Tina Gray, Global Head of Design and Innovation at Mayborn Group:

'The most important lesson I have learned is that some changes are a slow burn so the business has to be fully aware and supportive as to how long it may take for success to be visible.

'The risks are always assessed and then communicated as part of the business process, which are validated through various measures such as market share and value contribution. In a global business, it's also vital that trends are applicable to the markets you are launching in, so you may decide to exclude certain markets dependent on regional insights or you might launch to a different schedule depending on the maturity of the market.

'Proactively sharing results to internal and external stakeholders ensures i) there is a greater understanding of the importance of trends and ii) that capturing the learnings helps everyone each time the process is repeated.'[39]

Take the temperature

Companies sometimes want evidence that a new trend or idea is ripe before fully committing to a product launch. One way to build confidence is to conduct small-scale tests and trials before a full-scale market introduction. This approach allows companies to 'take the temperature' and gauge market reception with minimal risk.

In the words of the great business consultant Jim Collins, 'Fire bullets, then cannonballs'.[40]

Running trial quantities and batch testing a new idea might usually be the domain of merchandisers and

---

39   Interview with Tina Gray conducted on 24 January 2024 for the purpose of this book
40   J Collins and MT Hansen, *Great by Choice: Uncertainty, chaos, and luck – why some thrive despite them all* (HarperBusiness, 2011)

buyers, but it works in the favour of trend leaders, too, allowing you to evidence the appetite for a new trend, adjust your strategy if necessary, and provide some confidence to the business that the market is ready.

There are all sorts of ways a brand or retailer can use sampling to get a measure of how ready their customer is to experience a new trend. Sampling can include producing short runs to test the market readiness for a new product, through to running personalised, trackable campaigns (such as L'Oréal's virtual make-up try-on that allows customers to test thousands of shades of lipstick using augmented reality before they buy).

By analysing the data from sampling campaigns, retailers and brands can create a feedback system to gauge consumer mood and build confidence in a new idea or trend before fully investing.

Testing a new product or idea is not without its challenges, and it is important not to frame it as an exact science. You can run a test in which your proposed new idea sells out in twenty-four hours – but this success outpaces your supply chain, and you can't quickly access more stock. Or you can run a test in which the response is lukewarm and lose confidence in the idea, only to find a few short weeks later that the market appetite is red hot.

We've all been in stores in sale season and seen row upon row of a product that has failed to resonate with the consumer for whatever reason. Over-confidence, over-investment, and probably, somewhere behind the scenes, a team of people sitting in weekly sales meetings listening to the excruciating truth that the product they backed has spectacularly failed. Usually, under the surface of this scenario, sits some unchecked personal preferences, unvalidated trends or a lack of understanding about their customer and their readiness for this trend or new idea.

It's not to say that all of this can be avoided, but it is most certainly the case that in the world's best businesses, there is a sensible approach to taking the temperature before launching a product at mass scale.

I once worked with a company that was first to market with an innovation – the bifold concertina patio doors we are all now familiar with. They tested it for two years with no response from their customers and then shelved the invention, only to see the (unpatented) concept explode a year later in multiple markets in Northern Europe. The bifold door market was valued at ten billion dollars in 2024 and yet the company that invented it didn't make a dollar from it. Being first to market can be a case of holding your nerve, but what appetite has your company got for waiting? If you're too soon, how long will you be prepared to wait for your customer to catch up?

By the time you're at the trial phase, a trend leader will have done a lot of work to research, ideate and prove the concept, so it's important that, whether a trial succeeds or fails, you are clear about precisely what is and is not working.

It's important that you:

- Don't get into the habit of testing every new idea – it won't be financially or organisationally feasible, but over-testing also takes away some dynamism from the process, and over-relying on testing slows business decisions down.

- Clearly define the rationale behind your trial – is it to test an idea with a new prospective audience, or to test your customers' appetite for a new material, colour, motif or design aesthetic?

- Remember that a test can fail, but the trend can still go on to have a huge impact on your market. How long is your business prepared to wait? What's the tolerance level for a lacklustre market response?

- Continually communicate to your stakeholders that a progressive company must stay relevant, which means having the courage to take some managed risks.

- Understand that innovation and risk go hand-in-hand, but that risks can be managed.

- Persuade the business to communicate its relationship with failure. What is the company narrative when a new idea fails? How might this shape or hinder the desire to pursue future innovations?

By following these guidelines and maintaining a balanced approach to trend activation, companies can manage the inevitable risk of innovation.

The Timeless/Timely Index™

In business, trends are used to fuel innovation, which has been proven to be a critical driver of long-term success. However, it's important to strike a balance between the ratio of new product development (NPD) and your core offer that provides stability for your company.

The Timeless/Timely Index is a useful tool to help you understand the product range split that will deliver the most value for your business.

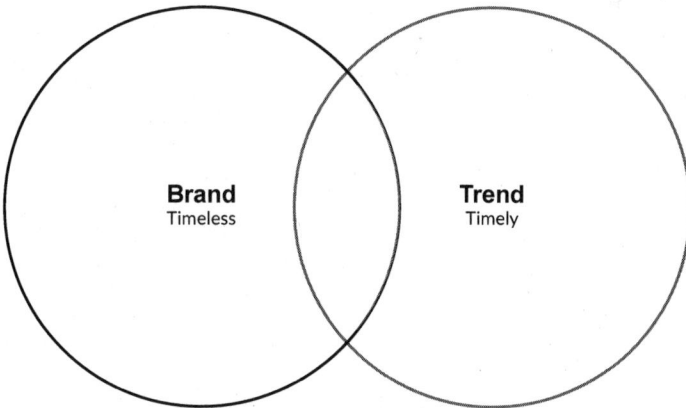

The Timeless/Timely Index™

- 'Timeless' refers to the enduring qualities for which you'll always be known. These may get refreshed every once in a while, but generally stay the same. They include the long-lasting perennial elements like design philosophy, core values and distinct aesthetic DNA that form the foundation of your brand and product portfolio.

- 'Timely' refers to the innovative, contemporary elements (such as NPD or marketing campaigns) that respond to evolving and emerging customer wants, needs and market changes.

Left to their own devices, most corporations would ideally opt to lean on the same core products that never change, year in, year out. However, the reality is that change happens, and doing the same thing over and over again isn't enough to achieve or maintain relevance. Progressive brands and retailers work hard to get the balance right between timeless and timely elements.

Whether you have a tangible end product or not, you'll want to have something fresh to say to your audience to remain visible and timely. Even Coca Cola (who have essentially sold one recipe in a couple of formats for over a century) take staying relevant extremely seriously. You will not see a huge change year on year in their timeless core product, but they work persistently with trends to inform their marketing and messaging to ensure they reflect the evolving needs and tastes of their audience.

If you're in the consumer products business, you're likely having to craft several product ranges, each with a different balance between timeless products and timely ones. Some companies are as specific as setting an 80/20 directive, so that 80% of the range must consist of core product, and 20% is 'newness'. For context, in 2024, LEGO alluded to the fact that their previous year's success was down to their portfolio mix with 48% of their product range classified as new product.[41]

A company that makes lamps and lighting might work to an 80/20 ratio of Timeless versus Timely (or Core versus NPD), because the market doesn't tend to have a high replacement cycle and the end customer buys these products expecting them to last five to ten years. A company making products with a shorter replacement cycle, such as birthday cards, might have a 20/80 ratio.

MEET THE TREND LEADER

Karen Thomas is Head of Home and Beauty at UK retailer Marks and Spencer:

'My job is to measure the mood of the nation, understand from customer data and insights what our M&S customer might want, and perpetually balance this with attracting new customers.

---

41 The LEGO Group, *The LEGO Group Annual Report 2023* (2024), www. lego.com/cdn/cs/aboutus/assets/blt7e9167f47da173a6/FINAL_ Annual_Report_2023.pdf, accessed 9 April 2025

'To get the range balance right, we look at the frequency of spend, where we have the staple home items that the customer will only replace once in a while, in core areas such as bed sheets or pans. However, we still drive frequent updates through impulse categories or high replacement categories to things like candles, vases and cushions to keep customers coming back. It's about balancing risk and measuring where you need to take risks to keep things fresh and interesting.'[42]

A company that relies too heavily on core 'timeless' product runs out of fresh things to say to their audience. It's not advisable to rely too heavily on timely product either, which can create a high-risk trading environment that comes to rely on fads rather than trends. You need to get the balance right to hit your commercial objectives, stand for something meaningful and have something new to say in the market.

There is another interplay between timeless and timely to consider. You must select trends that fit well with your timeless qualities. It will be immediately obvious to the consumer if you select trends that are off-brand and clash with the essence of what you're about.

A good exercise is to take a current trend and layer that over your company's values to see whether they fit. Take, for example, toy brand Mattel's core value promise to 'embrace all perspectives and strive for

---

42 Interview with Karen Thomas conducted on 10 October 2023 for the purpose of this book

diversity and inclusion'. To operate in alignment with that value, designers at Mattel need to seek out and act upon trends that promote this value.

It's always worth taking the time to get on the same page and talk with your stakeholders about how product ranges ought to be structured to best serve the business, category and, most importantly, the customer.

Using the Timeless/Timely ratio, ask yourself the following clarifying questions:

- Do you have company-wide agreement on how much newness your business needs to thrive?

- Does the ratio differ for different categories or departments?

- Can you get a sense of how your competitors segment their ranges?

Ensure you schedule an annual review to determine if any of your indexes need a refresh in order that you remain as adaptive and responsive as possible.

Reflection and action points

1. Take the Timeless versus Timely model template above. Workshop this with each product division and team. Look at past product ranges – what are your observations? Do different teams and

categories work to different percentages? Are
they doing so for the right reasons? Are they
leaning towards Timeless because they are afraid
to try new things?

2. For every trend, make sure you list out and label
a handful of 'calculables' – these are diarised
events like movie releases, the Olympic Games,
books to be published etc – for every trend. Make
sure each trend has a solid grounding in different
areas, for example food, architecture, technology
and literature. The more anchored the trend, the
better. Watch out though – a trend you can find
lots of grounding for is likely already established
and is about to happen!

3. Create a budget for commissioning a digital
regional nuances reference guide, helping you
store everything you know about a region's
culture, tastes and influences to help inform
your designers and marketing teams. Include
any 'watch out' warnings for words, phrases,
colours or motifs that might be found upsetting,
unappealing or illegal.

SEVEN

Principle Five: Validate Your Trends

Theories, ideas, imagining and hypotheses are the language of trend forecasting. While a trend expert can feel comfortable in this world of fluidity, other colleagues – who perhaps are used to leaning on hard facts to make their decisions – will need to be catered to in a particular way if you want to get them on board.

In this chapter, we will explore when and how to use data to back a trend and help stakeholders feel more reassured and comfortable about new ideas.

Defining meaningful metrics

At the start of the trend-forecasting process, you won't find many data points to reinforce your narrative or hypothesis, but data can serve as a powerful tool to support you later on. It's important to be absolutely clear about why the business is invested in any given trend and align your metrics to the business goal. What is it you need your trend to deliver to the business? Is there more to it than sales performance?

There are two instances where data is useful:

1. To back a trend in the early stages – adding weight to a hypothesis or theory

2. To measure the success of a trend once it's live

Let's look at each of these in detail.

Using data to back a trend in the early stages

Many companies rely heavily on data-driven decision making, often requesting concrete evidence to back up speculations about the future. As a trend builds momentum in the market, it will become easier to find evidence of its emergence and data points will increasingly become available to you. Being able to point to these and share them with your stakeholders is good practice and builds faith among your colleagues that the change you anticipated is starting to show signs of arriving.

It's important to manage your stakeholders' expectations from the start and let them know that, as soon as there is data available to support a trend, it will be shared with them. It's best to share this data in an organised way – a monthly, quarterly or biannual report that tracks the data signals of how and where a trend is emerging.

For example, your report might include:

- Qualitative data on when consumers with a Maven or Early Adopter mindset start to pick up on your trend

- A visit to a trade show to take photographs of any products or product characteristics you spot that mirror your trend

- Monitoring popular search terms linked to your new trend to demonstrate an emerging appetite for it

- Setting up a Google alert to inform you when new material associated with your trend gets published – everything from academic journals to magazine articles count as evidence of an emerging new movement

As these signals grow in number over time, you will notice that the sources will become less niche and more mainstream as the trend approaches full fruition. Be sure to articulate this to your stakeholders to manage their expectations. Don't forget that the more directional your trend is, the less measurable data there will be to support it.

Using data to measure a trend's performance

The commercial definition of a successful trend for a multinational corporate is mass-market uptake. This means a trend must be visible to over 70% of consumers, not just something a handful of consumers can experience in cool districts in major cities, but something that reaches out into suburbs, towns and onto the shelves of local stores everywhere.

There are many commercial aspects you can measure and use as key performance indicators (KPIs) when you want to know if a trend is successful, such as:

- Volume of sales
- The rate of sale or sell-through (how quickly it is selling)
- Press coverage
- Social media coverage

WATCH OUT

Trend leaders need to be mindful of how success and failure are reported. When a company has poor trend measurement tools, it can make it look like the trend failed when really there might be another reason behind the failure, such as poor stock availability or a delayed shipment from a supplier meaning the product didn't arrive in time to meet customer demand.

I've even known a supermarket report that a fashion trend failed, only to discover on closer inspection that the collection had never left the stockroom due to an unexpected heatwave which saw the business allocate shop floor space for disposable barbeques and paddling pools instead! This was a savvy commercial decision, but it led to the failure of the fashion collection and it wasn't clear at first why.

Taking control of your own set of metrics is the best way to get clarity on how trends are performing.

When to ask the customer

All of the FTSE 500 companies I've worked with engage in some kind of market research, but there's a vast difference in how the most innovative trend leaders use it. To remove the risk of launching a new product, companies often feel that conducting market research to get customer feedback is a surefire way to eliminate a negative market reception. It can feel like you're mitigating a risk, but I've seen this approach backfire so many times.

If Ben and Jerry's had asked people what their favourite ice cream flavours were, they would have said strawberry, chocolate and vanilla. Instead, Ben and Jerry's became globally renowned for their unique flavours and wouldn't have enjoyed such success if they had built their business on market research.

Quantitative data can offer generalisations. Imagine if, at the time of launch in 1984, Ben and Jerry's ran a poll that said that 75% of respondents thought that strawberry ice cream sounded preferable to Cookie Dough flavour. Would they have proceeded despite the 'evidence'? This is not to say that you never want to hear what your customer has to say, it's just that it can interfere with your innovation process and stop you from driving progressive change. Ben and Jerry's would not have become one of the world's most distinctive ice cream brands generating sales of $951 million.[43]

Using market research or customer focus groups to innovate and validate something new is flawed in one simple way – you are asking the customer 'will you like this product in two years' time?' and of course they don't have a reliable answer to that.

---

43   Statista, *Leading Ice Cream Brands in the United States in 2023, Based on Sales* (2023), www.statista.com/statistics/190426/top-ice-cream-brands-in-the-united-states, accessed 9 April 2025

It's your job as trend leader to anticipate what your customer will want, and craft your offer accordingly. The best trend leaders are in tune with their audience's shifting, evolving tastes, but don't rely on asking them *now* what they want *next* as an innovation strategy. In the words of Steve Jobs, co-founder of Apple Inc.:

> 'Some people say give the customers what they want, but that's not my approach. Our job is to figure out what they're going to want before they do. I think Henry Ford once said, "If I'd ask customers what they wanted, they would've told me a faster horse." People don't know what they want until you show it to them. That's why I never rely on market research. Our task is to read things that are not yet on the page.'[44]

So, when should you ask the customer?

Profiling Mavens

One great way to become attuned to your audience's wants and needs is to build a relationship with the people who influence them. New attitudes, values and behaviours start to emerge within a small influential group at first – I refer to them as Mavens, we met them earlier on in Chapter Five. They influence

---

44   W Isaacson, *Steve Jobs* (Simon & Schuster, 2011)

the agenda, and what they think, feel and do trickles down to mainstream consumers.

If you really want to know what your future customers will think, ask the Mavens. Inviting them into the conversation – via market research, focus groups or interviews – can be a great way of anticipating which values or behaviours may be on the horizon line for more mainstream customers.

The objective here is not to persuade them to buy from you or to align your products with meeting their specific needs. The intention of listening to what Mavens have to say is to tap into a more directional mindset and find out what is bringing them joy, infuriating them, and driving their behaviours.

Mavens will potentially never be the kind of person to buy from a mass-market brand, but that's not the goal of this exercise. Their rich, transformational thinking and desire to drive change is what's interesting, and the trend leader's role is to assess whether this has the capacity to influence what your customer thinks.

Back in 2012, I went on the hunt for Mavens that were serious about reducing their eco-footprint on behalf of a personal care brand. These Mavens were so serious, in fact, that they lived off-grid lifestyles. These were individuals who were doing everything they could to leave as light a footprint on Earth as possible.

At the time, a negative narrative had been building about the damage being done by single-use plastic packaging. This heightened awareness prompted this personal care brand to explore how it might take more eco-friendly action.

After interviewing eco-Mavens about their approach to personal hygiene, I detailed the lifestyle choices of these families and mapped out how their concerns shaped their mindset and decisions. I shared insights with the brand through qualitative data that helped them see how these seemingly extreme attitudes and behaviours could build momentum and begin to influence their mainstream consumers. Among the many fascinating and resourceful behaviours of the Mavens was how they had replaced their reliance on branded and bottled shampoo with making their own organic 'naked' (unpackaged) solid shampoo bars.

Over a five-year period, I tracked it from a new, niche Maven behaviour to mainstream acceptability. In 2018, high-street cosmetics brand Lush hit the headlines when they sold 12,000 solid shampoo naked bars in forty-eight hours, igniting mainstream interest in the new format. By 2022, the zero-waste 'naked shampoo' market was valued at almost two hundred million dollars.

WATCH OUT

Don't make the assumption that Mavens are always an elite or activist group. They are simply people who are prepared to solve problems for which they haven't found an adequate solution. I once worked with a value retailer who profiled 'cleaning Mavens' – people who cleaned high-spec homes and offices for a living and wanted the very best performing products to use every day. The knowledge these Mavens shared with the retailer enabled them to fuel their innovation pipeline.

How might you connect with the Mavens who are influencing your business or market?

- Conduct some observational research to profile your Mavens. Who are they? Where are they? What do they think, feel and do?

- Issue a call-out to ask Mavens to engage with you and show them you want to listen to drive positive change. Think about how you will reward them for their time in a way that is meaningful for them.

- Think carefully about how you frame them up to your business. Do your stakeholders understand enough about how influence spreads to be able to listen to and respect what Mavens have to say?

Evaluating your accuracy

A willingness to evaluate your accuracy will build credibility and trust among your stakeholders. By the time a trend hits the market, you will have been communicating clearly and consistently with your stakeholders about how trends work, why you've picked a particular trend, what your rationale is for believing it will work, and why you consider your audience to be ready for it. It would be remiss of you to not report on how right or wrong you got it. It's a valuable bit of data to collect.

It's important to follow the same process whether a trend is successful for your business or not.

When a trend succeeds, you will need to explain to the business why it worked – it was due to a particular process of spotting change and having the confidence to back and invest in an idea. It's good practice to map the trend from your first weak signals, to growing evidence in niche markets, through to live examples of it in the mainstream market, which will reinforce belief in your process. The more evidence you collect of the trend living and breathing across multiple products and categories, the more you'll bolster confidence in your forecasting abilities.

The following questions will help you validate your trends:

- Did you pick up on the most commercially successful trends?

- Did you execute them authentically and in a way that aligns with your brand?

- Which trends have emerged in the market that you have missed? Were these on your radar and why did you not respond to them? Was it a purposeful choice or is there a hole in your trend spotting system?

- How did the trend perform for your business and did anything hinder this?

Trend tracking

One of the most effective ways to evaluate your trend-forecasting accuracy is to track the trend as it hits the market. When you're trend tracking, you're working in the present, scanning for evidence of a trend you researched and ideated some time beforehand, perhaps even years, but that can now be evidenced in the mainstream market. Great trend leaders understand the value of tracking a trend the entire way through its cycle and have a constant eye on the present market and how it's responding to change.

At TrendBible, we track every trend we forecast, and this helps our clients see what a trend looks and feels like once it lands across a multitude of sectors, categories and industries. To do this yourself, you can create a simple document with photos or screengrabs of products that reflect the trend, or you can use an app like Slack or Teams to create a live feed of evidence through which the whole company can share examples of products, news articles or marketing campaigns that demonstrate your trend has gone mainstream. It will also help your stakeholders see just how different a trend can look in the hands of another company with a different brand character, or perhaps one serving a different category or market to you.

When a trend fails

As a trend leader, your job is not to be right 100% of the time. It's to be someone who seeks to improve the way a company responds to change, and to record an honest account of how the company operates. Remember – having no foresight at all yields much worse results than trying new things.

Of course, a truthful evaluation of your accuracy will at times show that you went too early, or too late, or that your business adapted a trend in a way that made sense at the time but that affected the end result in a detrimental way. In a large company with many people involved, it's important to find the truth as to why an idea or trend failed, and it's easy for loose assumptions about why it failed to quickly be misconstrued as hard evidence. Perhaps one department thinks that the product wasn't priced correctly, and another believes that the colour wasn't quite right. Without fully knowing the reason why a product failed to meet expectations, it's impossible to improve the process for next time.

How to record your success/failure

It's always worth keeping a record of your initial concept and what your intentions were, and comparing this to the reality of the company's end product. An idea often gets morphed, diluted and compromised for all kinds of reasons as it makes its way through the process, where things like pricing strategy or health and safety regulations can alter the concept.

This is not about assigning blame, the role of the trend leader is to provide a clear and honest account of how the idea journeyed from concept to a final product, how it was marketed, sold and received. The trend leader has a duty to make sure all stakeholders can see the process, understand which decisions were made and why, and to create a continuous process for improvement from these findings.

Here are some questions to ask to stress-test your process:

- Did the end product reflect your initial intentions? If not, were the decisions that altered it fair and necessary? Did they impede or improve its chances of success?

- Have we accurately evaluated failure? Are we sure about exactly what elements made it fail?

- What could you have controlled better about the essential components, language and narrative of the trend? Were you clear about what must remain intact?

- Which other companies produced a great response to this trend, and how has this been received by the customer and the press? How does the output differ to what you launched and when you launched it?

- Is there a point in the process at which key decision makers in the business lose confidence in an idea?

- Did you lose the authenticity of a trend by paying too much attention to your own limitations, restrictions or rules?

Reflection and action points

1. It's important to measure the success of trends to ensure they are delivering value to the business and avoid misinterpreting the reasons for any failures.

2. There are various things you can measure when evaluating the success of a trend, including volume of sales, rate of sell-through, press coverage and social media coverage.

3. Creating your own set of metrics for measuring trends is important to ensure that success and failure are reported properly. Consider measuring whether you want a trend

to drive a distinctive brand position or resonate with a new audience, and whether there is a 'hero' item in this trend you need to spotlight.

4. It's important to be clear about why your company is investing in trends and what you want them to achieve, beyond just sales performance.

5. Trend leaders need to be able to deliver a compelling rationale to the business to prove that a new idea is bankable, often when there is little tangible evidence in the present.

6. Trend leaders should always be mindful that a new trend is unlikely to be on the current customers' horizon, so you can't use their opinions as your only rationale to validate or reject a trend. Using customer focus groups as a method for predicting their future tastes and desires is fundamentally flawed.

7. The best trend leaders are in tune with their audience's shifting attitudes and tastes before behaviours are evidencable. They are able to anticipate what customers will want next.

EIGHT

Principle Six: Build Belief

So much of a trend leader's work is persuading people to believe in something new and then to act upon that belief. As the person responsible for bringing trends to your organisation's attention, your colleagues' and stakeholders' belief in you is critical.

Great trend leaders are well practised and confident when talking about trends. They understand that it's as much about *how* they say things as it is *what* they are saying.

A trend leader's job is to inspire belief and inspire action. It's typical for a trend leader to see a future others can't yet see, and it's not until growing evidence of that future begins to emerge in the real world that other stakeholders really start to believe in it.

By then, it can be far too late to act with any true conviction, the cost of which is lacking relevance with your customer.

This chapter will help you build your self-belief first. It will help you think about how to feel confident and comfortable in your own ideas first, and then we'll explore how you can persuade and influence your stakeholders. We'll also cover how to deal with any scepticism so that you can feel confident when challenged.

Building your trend leader profile

The position of trend leader is uniquely influential and can have a profound impact that spreads far and wide. You have the power to influence business decisions that can reach people all over the world. Never underestimate the power of a trend leader's work, which can shape someone's sense of self for the better, inspire new behaviours, break old habits and create a sense of belonging.

No matter how small or incremental you may consider the changes you're making, there is always room to think a little deeper about the impact of what you're putting out into the world. The world needs more bold ideas and we need to take every opportunity within our control to lead positive change.

Here are some questions you can ask yourself to identify areas where you can have a greater impact:

- What kind of impact will your idea or product have, socially, culturally, environmentally?

- Who does it impact positively, and who does it impact negatively?

- List five instances where you've driven impactful change. What are you proud of?

- List five instances where you wish you'd done things differently. What impact did this make, and how would you approach it now?

- What gets in the way of you making more transformational change?

- If you were to imagine driving transformational change without any real-world limitations, what would you dream of doing?

While integrating trends into your leadership skillset takes time, it is a career-enhancing endeavour that elevates your professional reputation. Have you thought about what kind of change you want to be known for?

MEET THE TREND LEADER

During his career, former research fellow and serial innovator Professor Roy Sandbach OBE established his position as a trend leader by tenaciously driving new ideas through global business Procter and Gamble. Using his deep understanding of unmet customer needs, he created many impactful innovations for the 170-year-old business. In 2024, I interviewed Roy and asked him to share the story of one of his most memorable innovations that put him in the spotlight and propelled his career:

'Innovation is all about matching what's needed with what's possible for economic value or social good – or both. Matching "what's needed with what's possible" again and again (to become a serial innovator) isn't simple. Innovators need to be resilient.

'I worked out that virtually all of Procter and Gamble's fabric care turnover was from products used in the washing machine. Let's reframe that into an insight. It meant that in the lifetime of clothes, the company made money in less than 1% of their life. So, what could we do about making money during the rest of the time – for example, when the clothes were being worn?

'My next insight came, quite simply, from watching people. I spent a great deal of day-to-day time with our consumers, looking at their life and not just their washing. I found "clothes crises" at every turn. But the worst? Spilling coffee or ketchup or wine – or anything – on shirts and tops during the day.

'Next, I needed an idea. I took a highlighter pen from my desk, emptied it and filled it with proprietary stain removal solution, creating what I referred to as a "stain pen".

I started to talk to pen makers and simultaneously began to work in the lab on the formulation. Months later, the patents were written and filed, and the prototypes were ready for testing. However, the company wasn't convinced. There was already a stain removal wipes category, and it was small. Of course, I knew my innovation was different.

'It took years, but after hundreds of discussions with business leaders and tests with consumers, we were on our way, with a new-to-the-world product called Tide-to-Go. We had matched "what's needed with what's possible".

'It has made hundreds of millions of dollars for the business. CNN called it a "must-have fashion item". It was the first ever Procter and Gamble product to be advertised during the Super Bowl halftime. It was included in the Oscar nominees' goodie bag and has even been to the International Space Station as part of the Mars expedition research programme. Yes, astronauts do need to clean their clothes!

'The pen is still around sixteen years later, on the shelves in the USA, and on Amazon everywhere in the world.'[45]

Articulating your future vision with conviction

As a trend leader, you are a conduit through which a trend flows, but you also get to shape it and host vital conversations about its trajectory. Challenge yourself to envision transformative change, and don't be afraid to think boldly and ask yourself, 'Is this business really thinking big enough?'

---

45 Interview with Roy Sandbach conducted on 25 February 2025 for the purpose of this book

This role can be particularly difficult when you find yourself as a key decision-maker in high-stakes situations, especially when championing an idea that lacks widespread support. In these moments, successful trend leaders rely on a combination of thorough research, effective communication and a well-constructed case for impending change.

They also learn to trust their intuition, recognising it as a distillation of years or even decades of experience, while always backing their insights with solid evidence. This balanced approach allows them to navigate the sometimes-solitary path of pioneering new ideas and driving meaningful transformation.

Becoming the face of your business

Strong trend leaders are good at building their visibility outside of the company. The most effective trend leaders are prepared to advocate for their work publicly and take the opportunity to talk about their company's approach to innovation and change, speaking with the press or being featured in company marketing.

Building your profile more publicly outside the organisation is also a really good way for getting internal buy-in for your ideas. In-house PR teams are usually keen to promote you as a brand ambassador, and trends can be extremely press-worthy territory, so you can maximise this opportunity to build your own personal profile. The best trend leaders devote time to packaging up some press-ready trend content that can be shared. My favourite examples of this are Pinterest's highly anticipated annual trend reports, Pantone's Colour of the Year and LEGO's World Play Day.

How might you spotlight the ways that you are driving positive change in your business?

Making your compelling argument

Before you begin to talk about trends in your business, it's important to build your own confidence. You can make a start by quietly building your knowledge so that you feel confident and informed before you open up a conversation with your colleagues about introducing a trend-forecasting process to the business.

Start by evaluating your own trend leadership skillset with our Trend Leader Skills Assessment Tool. This will help you identify your strengths and weaknesses and will signpost you to a series of educational tools and resources to help fill any knowledge gaps you may have.

Find the root of your compelling argument

Next, look for a data point, or a pivotal moment of change in your business or market. Perhaps you have identified an area in which your business is underperforming against the competition, or a place where it is weak and exposed to failure. This is a good place to begin to link a live business problem to a better understanding of the future consumer.

For example, you might identify a point at which the company is potentially missing the opportunity to make money, like Roy Sandbach (who we just met) did with Procter and Gamble when he realised their laundry care products only made money from 1% of clothes' lifetime. Or you may identify a fork in the road where a customer is being drawn towards a new style, like the story of the Chinese brand we met in Chapter Six, who found their domestic customer suddenly drawn towards a European aesthetic. Build a compelling statement that will pique the interest of your leadership team by first identifying a problem that needs to be solved or an unmet need that needs to be catered to.

Conducting the trend audit covered in Chapter Three is a good place to spot a root issue or problem that needs to be solved, or you could investigate your competitors' outputs to see which trends they have activated, and compare this to that of your own business. Once you have identified a compelling problem to solve, you can use this as your core argument for why the business needs to work on understanding the future consumer. This proactive approach is much more powerful than seeking permission (and asking for the associated budgets) to initiate a trend-forecasting process.

Open the conversation

Faith Popcorn, futurist, author and founder of consulting firm BrainReserve once said, 'The challenge of Futurism isn't in seeing it. It's in convincing people to embrace and act on it.'[46]

It doesn't matter what flavour of futures you're bringing into your business; whether it's trend forecasting, strategic foresight or futurism, it will be challenging to introduce them to the uninitiated.

Making the first step towards having a conversation about bringing a trend-forecasting process into your business can feel daunting at first, but you don't have to implement everything from this book at once. The key is to bring your team along on the journey, helping them envision the future you see. Change can bring a whole range of responses from your team – there will be those who are invigorated by it and those who find it difficult. It can be frustrating when others lack confidence in your vision simply because they cannot yet see what you see. To navigate these challenges, first conduct a Stakeholder Analysis using the template

---

46   F Popcorn, 'The Nostradamus of Marketing reveals what the future really holds', Faith Popcorn's BrainReserve (8 January 2021), https://faithpopcorn.com/trendblog/articles/the-challenge-isnt-in-seeing-it, accessed 9 April 2025

in the resource toolkit that accompanies this book to help you evaluate priorities across different teams.

MEET THE TREND LEADER

Karen Thomas, Head of Home and Beauty at Marks and Spencer had this to say when I interviewed her in 2023:

'Visionary designers want to drive innovation but sometimes they are ahead of the curve and the leadership team can't see it yet. As brand guardian, it's my job to balance both of those views and do what's right for the Marks and Spencer customer.

'Your intuition might be strong, but to open the conversation around a new trend, you'll need to make your case for change using tangible evidence, perhaps referencing other aspirational brands who are driving a unique and compelling offer or pointing to other markets where they are adapting to new trends.'[47]

The conduit to more

You are the conduit – the person who can open the door for your colleagues to learn about trend forecasting and how to anticipate the needs of the future consumer. You want to be prepared for any eventuality and anticipate questions and resistance as much as possible. You have to do the groundwork to prepare an organisation for using and responding to trends.

---

47   Interview with Karen Thomas conducted on 10 October 2023 for the purpose of this book

Working with trends is not a one-time event, it's a cycle, so it's important to start small and build from there, knowing that you will soon have to go back to the business to present more new ideas as your customer and the world around the business continues to change.

Ask yourself these questions to help you interrogate your own thinking first:

- How do I know I'm right about this trend – have I gathered evidence?

- What language must I include and avoid in my presentation of this trend?

- How can I frame up previous successes to build trust ahead of introducing a new idea?

- Have I reminded everyone of my repeatable process, and the solid methodologies I'm using to draw these conclusions?

- Have I clearly connected the trend to the unmet needs, future behaviours, habits and lifestyles of our future customer?

Once you have demonstrated that the key to solving business problems lies in a better understanding of your future consumer, you will have captured the attention of your stakeholders, and you can begin to explore bringing some trend intelligence into your business.

Dealing with trend sceptics

Not everyone you run into in business is going to be as keen on trends and change as you are. In fact, if you haven't already been met with a healthy dose of scepticism, be prepared! Those who are sceptical about trends will challenge you, and voices from within your company will suggest that trends are for other types of companies, trends are dangerous, trends are not the way to unlock a stable future. You will need to be able to work alongside these people and be able to function, stay motivated and maintain your self-belief.

There are all sorts of reasons why scepticism becomes an obstacle. Futures work, by its very nature, brings your relationship with ambiguity into question, some people are simply characteristically more resistant to change, while others have a more pragmatic resistance, like an aversion to the cost of doing something new.

Many established trend leaders have stories about how difficult it can be to introduce trends to a company for the first time. Talita Di Iorio, Senior Consultant, formerly of Google, Meta and X, shared her advice during our interview in 2024:

> 'It's not uncommon to face scepticism.
> Sometimes, looking at past success stories can
> help: can you identify a past trend that had
> a similar pattern or movement, that wasn't

> supported by tons of quantitative data at the
> time, but was successfully leveraged by a
> brand that acted in the right moment?'[48]

Sometimes, a company just cannot build sufficient confidence in a trend to activate it. This often happens the first time a company is exposed to the trend-forecasting process. They get cold feet, and let the trend pass them by. The best thing you can do in this instance is to let it go, track the trend (using the trend tracking methods from Chapter Seven) and then, when the trend hits the market, use this as a case study to remind your company that they chose to opt out. Show them what opportunities they missed out on. It creates a sense of healthy FOMO (fear of missing out) next time around!

There are times when trends are weird, ridiculous and shocking. When this is the case, you're going to have a harder time convincing your colleagues that you need to invest in them. Over time, these ideas become less ridiculous, and we get used to them as we see them start to trickle into society. Think about when you first heard about drone usage moving from military use to commercial use, where they would be used by companies like Amazon to deliver our groceries. Or the first time you learned about self-driving cars. At first sight, these innovations sit within the realm of science

---

48   Interview with Talita Di Iorio conducted on 28 February 2024 for the purpose of this book

fiction, but within a short timeframe they become normalised and begin to infiltrate everyday life.

When faced with doubt or scepticism, ask yourself these questions:

- Is your audience truly sceptical, or just new to working with future trends?

- Point to a trend your company has missed but that a competitor seized upon successfully. Can you guide your colleagues to unpick what process, culture and mindset might have led the competitor to act with confidence?

- Before any trend presentations, have you educated your audience on common misconceptions and myths in the world of future trends to avoid unhelpful interruptions or public displays of scepticism?

MEET THE TREND LEADER

Geoff Sanderson, greetings industry expert, founder of Jungle Studio, and former Creative Director at Moonpig and Hallmark:

'In my career in the greetings card industry, we used trend forecasts to evolve core best-sellers and identify newness or points of difference to our product ranges in a saturated market. This also gave us commercial and marketing differentiation over our rivals – adding long-term value as well as being first to market where they couldn't. What helped the companies I worked in understand the value of trends was that they enabled the leadership team to see the consumer overlay. They could tell an investor or finance person the *why* behind a particular product or idea and why a product mattered. The realisation that trends were what kept us relevant with the customer and gave the rationale behind the product was a revelation.

'At Moonpig, we started with a test phase – we commissioned a trend forecast for one season, then another season. Then we decided we needed trend intelligence four times a year and our trend presentations began to get taken seriously. The whole team looked forward to those kick-off meetings and we put them right at the heart of our process.

'In my career, I've experienced management teams that worried about the cost of bringing in an external trend resource, but once they realised trend forecasting was giving them these massive clues about the future direction we could go in it gave them the confidence to engage with it.'[49]

Ultimately, you are looking to create some proof that you can spot and back the right trends, and get some agreement from your leadership team that they will show support for new ideas and invest in creating the right environment for them to flourish.

---

49 Interview with Geoff Sanderson conducted on 20 December 2023 for the purpose of this book

TREND LEADER

Establishing your internal ambassador network

Trend leadership need not be a one-person crusade, in fact, often the most enjoyable part of the role is taking others on the journey with you. You'll need to improve the visibility of your mission with two key groups of stakeholders to get maximum support and impact.

Identify a champion

Unless you are on the board of directors or the C-Suite, or are part of the senior leadership team, you will need to identify someone who will champion you at that level to raise your profile and galvanise support for your ambition to introduce a trend-forecasting process. Senior-level stakeholders such as design directors may have personal experience of introducing trends into a business before, or there may be other non-executive board members with this experience who can support and mentor you.

You will need director-level engagement to drive transformational change, but before you make a case for that, it is useful to identify a champion to help advise and give you feedback on:

- Your trend audit findings – have you found a compelling reason (an opportunity or a risk) to bring this to the board's attention?

- The company's strategic goals – do your audit findings align or conflict with these? Is there anything your champion can share that you haven't considered?

- Your proposed approach to introducing trend forecasting to the business

- How open those in the C-Suite are to understanding future trends and the future consumer, and if there is any appetite to explore this opportunity

As well as communicating and collaborating well with senior leadership teams and the board, to get a trend off the ground and alive inside a business requires you to make it matter to an even broader network of people. One of the reasons trends get stuck, stall or die inside a business is because the trend doesn't get activated among a big enough group of people.

Appoint a Trend Ambassador network

When we work with a company, part of our process at TrendBible is to find out who is going to be internally responsible for execution. Even in companies where there is a strong investment in trend material and the designers are trend-literate, something falls down between knowing what the trends are and doing something meaningful with them.

Commissioning external trend intelligence in the form of a presentation or trend subscription alone won't maintain sufficient momentum for a trend to keep moving towards fruition. Even with the best of intentions, and a trend that everyone agrees at the beginning should not be missed, it can fail to be activated.

Knowing what the trends are is only half of the job – knowing what to do with them and keeping them alive all the way through your design process into your marketing campaigns and onto the shelf is where you need internal team members to take responsibility. This is why I recommend establishing a Trend Ambassador network to help you reach the execution stage and ensure a good pace is maintained.

Trend Ambassadors are a group of internally recruited team members charged specifically with keeping trends alive and tracking their progress. They are trained to have a deep understanding of what the trends are and what they will look like when they are delivered. They are the go-to support network for the trend leader and also for your designers and marketers, reporting back progress and blockages in the pipeline to the trend leader.

It's worth mentioning that Trend Ambassador is an additional role beyond their day job, so they are usually recruited from the design or marketing teams but have clear responsibilities at key times in the year.

There is usually no shortage of people wanting to nominate themselves as Trend Ambassadors, but it's important to apply a strong commitment to diversity when recruiting to be able to see a trend from a variety of perspectives. Trend Ambassadors help amplify your trend work and can act as feet on the ground inside your business, helping to signpost team members towards trend intelligence and encouraging them to collaborate.

I have recruited and placed a number of Trend Ambassador networks inside brands and retailers and have found this approach works incredibly well. I've seen it be the difference between a brand that is able to respond to change, and one that is not.

Reflection and action points

1. Expect scepticism when you're talking about trends and introducing change.

2. Remember that change is sometimes shocking and ridiculous and that will prompt more challenge!

3. Good-quality trend forecasting is a group effort and involves a network of people.

4. Consider appointing Trend Ambassadors to keep trends alive and track progress within the business.

5. Take opportunities to talk internally and externally about trends. Make sure you tell your internal PR team that you're up for being approached by the press to talk about trends.

6. Craft a compelling statement by identifying a problem that needs to be solved or an unmet need that needs to be catered to.

Conclusion

Throughout this book, we have explored the nuances of trend leadership – why it matters, how to cultivate it and the profound impact it can have on businesses and society.

By demystifying the process of trend forecasting, my hope is that I've empowered you with the confidence to become the master of trends and to host a conversation about how your company prepares for the future.

Trend leadership is a wonderful training ground for some of the most in-demand leadership qualities, and enhances your ability to think strategically, to motivate and influence others, and to develop your resilience. It is accessible to those of you working inside a retailer or brand and it is a gateway to other related fields such as strategic foresight, strategy and innovation.

The impact a trend leader can have on their audience should not be underestimated. You are uniquely positioned to influence millions of people and encourage them to act in new ways. Use your position to make the world a better place – incrementally at first, by making one influential decision at a time. Could your project or idea be greener, take your customer towards a healthier life, or protect the environment in some way? Secondly, I urge you to think transformationally. Not just foresee, but to actively shape a better future. What kind of change might you drive?

Key takeaways from the book:

1. **The importance of vision:** Understanding what a better future looks like is pivotal. Aligning this vision with corporate and personal values enables trend leaders to drive meaningful change.

2. **Building an airtight process:** Establishing a systematic approach to trend forecasting ensures that trends are not just identified but also appropriately activated within the business to meet the needs of your future consumers.

3. **Cultivating curiosity:** Encouraging a culture of curiosity and openness to challenge is essential for innovation. It allows trend leaders to stay

ahead, constantly questioning and adapting to the shifting social and cultural landscape.

4. **Harnessing data and insights:** Using data intelligently enables you to make informed decisions, reducing risks and crafting strategies that resonate deeply with future market dynamics.

5. **Leadership and influence:** By becoming visible advocates for change within their organisations, trend leaders unlock new opportunities, not just for businesses, but for societal advancement.

Remember that the future does not merely unfold – it is actively created by the decisions we make today. The role of a trend leader is ever-evolving, demanding continuous learning and adoption. It is not just about responding to changes; it's about orchestrating them, leading the way in redefining what consumers desire and expect. It's about making informed, bold decisions that really challenge the status quo and drive progress. The opportunity to drive the change the world needs is in your hands.

Next steps

To continue your journey as a trend leader, I invite you to access exclusive resources designed to enhance your skills and understanding. Visit www.joannafeeley.com or scan the QR code at the end of the book to unlock the Trend Leader Toolkit that complements the insights from this book.

Further Reading

Collins, J and Hansen, MT, *Great by Choice: Uncertainty, chaos, and luck – why some thrive despite them all* (HarperCollins, 2011)

Elkington, J, *Cannibals with Forks: The triple bottom line of 21st century business* (Capstone Publishing, 1999)

Gladwell, M, *The Tipping Point: How little things can make a big difference* (Little, Brown and Company, 2000)

Kale, S, 'The mattress landfill crisis: how the race to bring us better beds led to a recycling nightmare', *The Guardian* (12 February 2020), www.theguardian.com/environment/2020/feb/12/mattress-landfill-crisis-recycling-nightmare, accessed 9 April 2025

Kesslen, B, 'Aunt Jemima brand to change name, remove image that Quaker says is "based on a racial stereotype"', *NBC News* (17 June 2020), www. nbcnews.com/news/us-news/aunt-jemima-brand-will-change-name-remove-image-quaker-says-n1231260, accessed 9 April 2025

RADAR, *Multiplayer Futures* (2024), www.radardao. xyz/multiplayer-futures, accessed 9 April 2025

Acknowledgements

T hanks go to those who helped me make the space required in my life to write a book. Running a business and raising a family have both required extra support, and I could not have written this book – or done much else in life – without the unwavering support of the below fantastic people.

First, thank you to my team at TrendBible. You really are the dream team and I consider myself so lucky to get to work with you all every day.

Huge thanks to Geoff Sanderson, Amelie Labarthe, Tina Gray, Karen Thomas, Professor Roy Sandbach, Talita Di Iorio, Elisabetta Stacchiotti, Alex Post Miller, Herb Kim, Dr Jo Gooding and Ruby Sommer for so generously sharing your amazing stories and insights with me.

Thank you to my beta readers Naomi Pollard, Carol Cloughton, Anna Ward, Peter Bell, Jo Ritzema, Ivan Hollingsworth and Harry Marsland for your clarity, encouragement and wisdom. It made all the difference and kept me going.

Thanks also to Laura Weaving at Duo Global Consulting for your collaboration and hard work on the behavioural study.

I would like to thank the whole team at Rethink Press for their guidance throughout this process.

Thank you to my parents, Anne and Ian, for their support through all my endeavours, and my sisters, Helen, Jennie and Carol for their unwavering encouragement and support.

To my wonderful sons, Aidan and Cameron, thank you for your patience, encouragement and interest in my book-writing process.

Lastly, the biggest thank you goes to my husband, Simon – ever patient, encouraging and quietly accepting of all my many projects and ideas. Thank you for all your support. I couldn't follow my dreams without you by my side.

The Author

Joanna Feeley is founder and CEO at TrendBible, a trend-forecasting agency specialising in the future of life at home. She has over twenty-five years' experience as a trend forecaster and consultant. Her models and advice in this book are based on her work advising brands, retailers and charities on what future audiences will think, feel and do.

Joanna writes and speaks about the future of life at home, and her insights have been published by *The Independent*, *Financial Times*, *The Guardian*, *Retail Week*, BBC Radio 4 and *Marketing Week*.

A multiaward winning businesswoman, Joanna was named as 'one of the new generation of female entrepreneurs' by think-tank Institute of Public Policy Research (IPPR), and was named Creative Entrepreneur of the Year in the Great British Entrepreneur Awards. She is a member of the Association of Professional Futurists.

To access tools, templates, resources, articles and podcasts go to www.joannafeeley.com or scan the QR code below.

🌐 www.joannafeeley.com

📷 www.instagram.com/trendbible

💼 www.linkedin.com/in/joanna-feeley-85919716/